RELATIONSHIP 1:1
The Genesis of Togetherness

RELATIONSHIP 1:1
The Genesis of Togetherness

Gavriel Goldfeder

Alternadox Press

Published by:

Alternadox Press
1805 Balsam Ave.
Boulder, CO 80304

Book design by Karen Sperry
Edited and Managed by Bruce Shaffer

All inquiries about this and other Alternadox publications should be addressed to:
Rabbi Gavriel Goldfeder
Kehillath Aish Kodesh
1805 Balsam Ave., Boulder, CO 80304
www.boulderaishkodesh.org
heyrabbi@gmail.com

ISBN: 978-0-9839051-0-3

Printed in the United States of America

www.alternadox.net

DEDICATION

To my wife, Ketriellah.
In celebration of the genesis
of our togetherness.

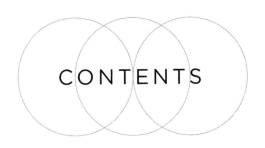

CONTENTS

ACKNOWLEDGMENTS

MY DEEPEST GRATITUDE TO A WIDE network of readers who have given me essential feedback on this work. In particular, Bruce Shaffer has continued to believe in me and support me through the process of writing, refining, and publishing this book. Joshua Levin has been a fabulous editor. Charlie Buckholz and Dr. Alan Morinis provided critical feedback at critical junctures. The good folks at Pekoe Sip House in Boulder have provided tea and warm smiles as I sat there every Wednesday, week in and week out. I am eternally grateful to my rabbis and mentors, including Rav Natan Greenberg, Rav Daniel Kohn, Rav Yehoshua Kahan, and Rav Eliezer Shore, who not only taught me how to learn, but how to think for myself. Most of all, I am grateful to my wife, Ketriellah, with whom I have experienced most of what this book discusses. I appreciate her willingness to allow me to write about our relationship so openly. Her wisdom is woven throughout these pages, explicitly mentioned only occasionally but always there.

INTRODUCTION

WE CAN READ THE TORAH AS the story of one lifetime. It begins in the Garden, a sort of primordial playground where all needs are taken care of and very little is expected of us. It ends at the banks of the Jordan River where we are expected to take care of ourselves. In between these two bookends are the various stages of life that constitute the journey. We find the family struggling for harmony in Genesis, engaging their purpose in Exodus, establishing structure in Leviticus, responding to the challenges to that structure in Numbers, and finally seeing the big picture in Deuteronomy. Read this way, as the story of a single life, the Torah is not only textured and evocative, but highly personal.

Genesis contains only a handful of laws. It is clear from the outset that the book is more about human development in the context of relationship than it is about legal structures. From Adam and Chava through Cain and Hevel and then onward all the way to Yosef and his brothers, we are confronted with people navigating issues of integrity, honesty, purpose, and cooperation amidst complex and challenging filial ties.

So the Torah, as a story of growing up, begins in Genesis as a story about relationships. Certain essential stages of consciousness and self-consciousness cannot emerge in isolation—they are irrevocably connected to the web of family. When we exit the foggy womb of unawareness, both literally and figuratively, our loved ones are there to greet us.

The family into which we are born—the container for our entry into this world—is a complex matrix of relationships. Even before we become conscious of ourselves and others, the complexities of those relationships have their effect on us. We are pushed and pulled by the particular brands of love and fear that permeate the household. Our open, undiscerning minds are flooded with old family stories, tones of voice, unspoken tensions, and explosions of emotion. We are taught our family's relational symphony—its particular mix of joy and anger, silence and yelling, resentment and forgiveness, disappointment and gratitude.

Family bonds define our earliest understanding of relationship, but they rarely provide us with what we need in order to become mature in relationship. The Torah tells us that marriage—our chosen, rather than given, family—is the context in which we truly grow. "Therefore, a man shall leave his father and his mother, and cling to his wife.[1]"

In marriage, the psychological material we brought with us from our family of origin will play out. There are additional factors in marriage that make more healing and growth possible than in our family of origin. Attraction, willfulness, and mature love each add to the potency and possibilities of our relational journey. However, even these cannot guarantee that marriage will fix any relationship damage we may have suffered growing up. We can give it a better chance, though, by understanding the effects that those earliest relationships had on us. At least we can understand the starting point from which we are entering our marriage.

The same parallels between filial ties and marriage relationships can be read in the book of Genesis. The characters' marriages segue naturally from their relationships with their other family members. We see hints of this: "And Yitzhak brought [Rivkah] to the tent of Sarah his mother, and he took Rivkah to him as a wife, and he loved her, and he was consoled from the [loss of] Sarah his mother." Another example: Just as Ya'akov is running away from his brother Eisav, who is trying to kill him, his father tells him, "Go to Padan Aram, to the house of Betu'el, your mother's father, and take from there a wife from among the daughters of Lavan, your mother's brother." And, another: "And Yosef named his first born Menashe, for 'G-d has helped me to forget my struggles and my father's house.'"

When we do look at the people and relationships that populate Genesis, we find that almost all of them seem broken—husbands and wives who deceive and manipulate each other, brothers and sisters who compete and sometimes kill each other, parents who chose favorites among their children, children who trick their parents. We would be hard pressed to find a single relationship in Genesis that is simple, clear, and loving from beginning to end.

That's good news, because *our* relationships are not simple and loving from beginning to end. If Genesis only offered us perfect relationships, we wouldn't learn about ourselves. As it stands, we can look at these people, their struggles, and the decisions they made to rectify their relationships, and we can enhance our own relationships—both given and chosen—accordingly.

The focus here, though, is on marriage–the most important chosen relationship. Marriage has great power to transform us. I know it's had this affect on me, and I've witnessed it do the same for many others. Indeed, I believe the very institution carries the capacity to make us truly human—patient, honest, aware, compassionate, humble. Obviously, though, it is not automatic. We need the guidance that comes from teachers, teachings, and our own experience. The Torah provides some of the best guidance that I know of, and I have set out here to open the door to some of what it can offer us.

YOU'LL NOTICE THAT I TREAT THE characters that populate the book of Genesis as people. This does not express the full complexity of my understanding of them, but it is an important piece of the puzzle. I also see them as archetypes, superheroes who were capable of changing the world they were born into through superhuman feats. They established the physical, emotional, intellectual, and spiritual foundations of the Jewish people in a world that was in many ways resistant to their project. Their actions had ramifications on many levels for thousands of years to come. They had a direct relationship to G-d that may be hard to fathom. But the Torah presents them as people. It gives us a peek into their struggles and invites us *ta shema*—to come and learn.

My intention is not to in any way denigrate them. If it seems like I am being harsh at times, I assure you it is only because I believe in their resilience as people and as characters. And any implied critique of their character and decisions is intended to highlight and praise their eventual triumphs and transformations.

IN THIS BOOK, I DRAW ON a variety of sources, ranging from the Genesis stories themselves to contemporary writers like Aviva Zornberg. There are passages from Talmud and Midrash, both of which feature ideas that were expressed by Jewish sages around two thousand years ago. I also draw on Rashi (the foremost medieval commentary on the Torah, who died in the year 1105) and other classic commentaries on the Torah. You will find reference to some of the Chassidic masters, from the Ba'al Shem Tov to Rebbe Nachman. And I have drawn on the writings of Rabbi Avraham Yitzhak HaCohen Kook, who was the first Ashkenazic Chief Rabbi of the pre-state of Israel, who died in 1935. My views are also informed by the ideas of contemporary writers on relationship such as David Deida and David Schnarch.

SOME GUIDANCE ON HOW TO ENGAGE with this book: The Torah was divided up into segments—each one is called a *parsha*. One *parsha* is read each week in synagogues across the denominational spectrum and around the world. Each chapter in this book revolves around one *parsha*, with the addition of Hanukkah, which falls during the reading of the book of Genesis. Each *parsha* may contain several stories or passages but can often be boiled down to one theme.

It would be useful, though not necessary, to read through the weekly Torah reading, even cursorily, before attempting to understand the corresponding chapter in this book. A basic familiarity with the story and its characters is assumed, and the reader might not fully grasp the concepts in this book without such familiarity. Easy-to-read translations are abundantly available.

However, I do not recommend that the reader necessarily try to read a chapter per week. If one or another chapter's ideas are compelling, a pause may be warranted to work on that particular theme or process before moving on. And it goes without saying that this book still applies even if the *parsha* being read that week in synagogues throughout the world is not in the book of Genesis.

I suggest that couples read this material together, which can help them establish a common vocabulary for the challenges they face together. Of course, it can also be read on one's own, or with a group of couples.

BEREISHIT

Genesis 1:1-6:8

*The world is created in six days; G-d rests on the
seventh day. G-d makes man, but with no partner.
After Adam encounters and names all the animals,
G-d casts him into a deep sleep, removing one of
his sides and making it into Chava. Adam and Chava
become "one flesh." They soon eat from the
Tree of Knowledge and are exiled from the Garden.*

TRANSITION

I MET MY WIFE AFTER TWO years of learning in *yeshiva*. Before I got married, every day was filled with 14-16 hours of Torah study and prayer—bliss! Life was stimulating and fulfilling. I had a sense of purpose and clear measures of success. Marriage was quite the contrast: I felt inadequate, fumbling and bumbling through many an interaction. Frankly, I was inexperienced at considering the needs of another person. I could learn a page of Talmud, but did not want to apply myself to Ketriellah's vocabulary, body language, moods, and rhythms. Given the discrepancy between being a pretty good *yeshiva* student and a fairly lousy husband, I chose to spend as much time as possible in the *yeshiva*, where I wasn't a dunce.

In *yeshiva*, my own interests, spiritual as they were, stood at the center of my world. It's still easy for me to continue to pursue my bliss and even insist that this pursuit be my priority. But when I take this position, I overlook the needs and desires of others, including my wife. I know that this is no way to live, at least not for me. I'm clear that the joys of togetherness are worth giving up the need to keep my personal interests as the sole priorities at the center of my world. Nothing I can accomplish on my own is as satisfying as building something together with my wife, so I am committed to learning how to be in relationship in a full and healthy way.

I have encountered many people who've been frustrated in their search for a partner. They wonder why they cannot find that special someone. It's a good question—they are talented, likeable, and hard-working. But potential partners are put off by the unconsciously delivered message: "I am perfectly fine on my own and emotionally self-sufficient. As long as my own needs and interests can stay firmly at the center of my world, I'd consider being involved with you." This message represents the inability or unwillingness to make the transition required by healthy relationship—letting go of our tight grip on our own self-importance and opening to the needs of the other and our shared pursuits.

ALONE IN THE GARDEN

This tension between self and relationship has been causing trouble since the Torah's first dynamic duo—Adam and Chava.[1] Their three-hour honeymoon came to a screeching halt when they ate from the Tree of Knowledge. You know that story. But what happened *before* Chava was created? Adam was a bachelor for two hours[2] before G-d declared that it was "not good for man to be alone." During those two hours, Adam had had a job: "And he brought [the animals] to Adam to see what he would call them, and whatever Adam called each creature, that was its name."[3]

The Torah has to tell us about that two-hour period so it can teach us about the dramatic, sometimes rocky transition from single life to married life. What were you like before you met your future spouse? Perhaps you had a clear sense of who you were and what you liked, and maybe even where your life was headed. Adam did. Then you got married, and suddenly things weren't so simple. Your dreams alone would cease to guide your future. Your tastes would no longer be the sole determinant for what ends up on the dinner table, the social calendar, or the TV. And that unimpeded sense of self would henceforth battle for survival in the crucible of intimacy.[4]

Why did you throw away all that autonomy? Because you needed to, like Adam needed Chava. It's a fact of life: "It is not good for man to be alone." Everything else in creation was pronounced "good," or even "very good." But aloneness is simply "not good." And all those pursuits—career, sense of self, personal preferences, even Torah study—need to be subject to negotiation for the sake of quelling that aloneness.

What, exactly, is wrong with aloneness? Our sages' answer is decidedly unromantic: If man is alone, he will think he is a god.[5] And you thought it was because of love!

It's not that our sages of old didn't believe in love. But they saw the roots of relationship penetrating far below simple attraction to a universal, existential need. Relationship allows us to do what we cannot do on our own: debunk the myth that we are gods. Deep down we want that. And we fall in love with the person who could make that grueling process fun and interesting.

Obviously, the "god complex" is not about imagining ourselves as all-knowing or all-powerful—after all, doesn't every aspect of the world around us, from politics to the weather, remind us endlessly that we are clearly not? Rather, it's about this false sense that *our* opinions, preferences, and needs are all that matter. And nothing dispossesses us of this illusion better than a good marriage, as our spouse's opinions, preferences, and needs may often conflict with our own. We vie for control of day-to-day decisions and the larger direction of our shared life. Indeed, relationship is the unique antidote for the god complex.

ISN'T THERE ANOTHER WAY?

We understand why it was not good for Adam to be alone. But why not make this second human a man? Adam #2 could have challenged Adam #1's god complex as well as any woman. So why make this new humanoid female—and attractive? Because G-d had another goal in mind: He did not want Adam to fight this new humanoid for territory or dominance. Rather, G-d wanted Adam to *seek out* this new person's companionship. He wanted Adam to *want* to be with her, to feel like he was missing something without her.

It certainly worked! When Adam first gazed upon Chava, his attraction to her was immediate and intense—what you may have felt when you met your future spouse. Adam was so overwhelmed that he didn't think to ask whether it was worth giving up being the star of the universe. He simply jumped off his own pedestal and stepped into relationship.

THE TIMELINE

There's more food for thought in our relation-creation story. If Chava was put there so Adam wouldn't mistake himself for a god, why didn't G-d just make two humans to begin with, like He did with all the other animals? Why this long, dramatic process, replete with aloneness and delusions of grandeur?

Clearly G-d wanted Adam to have some time alone, if only for a couple of hours, to sit with the very sense of all-importance that Chava would come to challenge and resolve. G-d wanted Adam to have his center-stage time, to be the king of all he surveyed, namer of animals, envy of the angels, to feel divine, unique, empowered, and important. And *then* G-d wanted that feeling to be deflated, or at least modified, by Chava's arrival.

Adam's story is common to all men and women. Each of us grows up as the most important occupant of our world. We spend two decades or more living in that story, building a sense of who *we* are, what *we* want to do, and what pleases *us*. And then our culture, our psyche, and our longing for partnership tell us that the *me*-world is not enough. It loses its lustre as we catch glimpses of fulfillment in a new world with different rules, responsibilities, and pleasures. We know we want to be there, in the love-world, but we are not necessarily happy about how much we need to leave behind.

A deep message is embedded in the story of Adam and Chava: G-d gives us time to cultivate our unique identity, power, importance, and divinity—everything Adam had before he met Chava. And then we are meant to get married, where the coin of the realm is humility, caring, compromise, and cooperation. Both of these experiences are real, valid, and important. Somewhere between alone-divine-complete and together-human-incomplete, our married life plays out.

WHEAT BECOMES BREAD

The verse that begins "it is not good for man to be alone" has an intriguing denouement: "...[therefore] I will make for him a helper against him." If a partner is a helper, why is she "against?" And if the partner is against, how is that helpful? Rabbi Yossi, one of the sages of the Talmud, was perplexed enough by the verse that he asked Elijah the Prophet himself what it meant. Elijah cryptically answered: "A man brings wheat. Can he chew wheat? He brings flax. Does he wear flax? Rather, she opens his eyes and sets him on his feet."[6]

This idea of a helper who is "against" gets fleshed out in the context of how strongly we cling to our pre-married lives. The wheat and flax that the man in the parable brings from the field seem to represent the character, skills, tastes, and qualities that each of us cultivates before we find each other. They are powerful and wonderful, but raw. They must be refined in order to take their place within a larger and more comprehensive picture.

If I can let go of my attachment to being the center of my world, all sorts of amazing possibilities open up. I can learn so much more about myself, can maximize the development of my talents, and can get better at relating to others beyond my household. Marriage challenges me to admit to needing another and to express my gratitude. It requires that I take full responsibility for my part in the relationship and holds me accountable when I don't. This is a formidable challenge, but the benefits are worth it. I was holding some raw wheat, and now, thanks to my wife, we've got bagels!

Did the man and woman in the parable even eat before they met each other? We might look back on our former lives and wonder how we were ever happy. Granted, we got our way a lot more, but the expanded possibilities and deeper satisfaction that come out of loving partnership make that old joy seem rather thin.

NO WHEAT = NO BREAD

Stubborn refusal to give up being the me-world is not the only way to sabotage the bread-making process. At the other end of the spectrum, some people are all too ready to give up everything, including their spine, in order to cooperate. They see their old lifestyle and interests as irrelevant, dead weight to be cast overboard in order to arrive at marital bliss as quickly as possible. That is not at all what I'm advocating for. It's not a healthy strategy, nor is it even possible.

We cannot just forget who we have been, though we can certainly try to stuff it under the rug.

Returning to Eliyahu's parable, the raw material that we bring to the relationship nourishes both of us. It is a big part of what attracted us to each other in the first place. And even the ingredients that don't initially seem tasty are part of the package and can't be separated out. I know a man who insisted he would never marry a woman who liked country music or disliked Woody Allen movies. If he now insisted that his wife toss out her Garth Brooks CD's, he'd be messing around with the very DNA of why he loves her. It would be like trying to cut out a single unattractive thread from an otherwise beautiful tapestry. It can't be done without ruining the whole thing. And if, on the other hand, he pretended to like her music, he would be messing with his own tapestry.

Most of us know people who try to give up essential aspects of who they are for the sake of a partner, but it ends up being to their mutual detriment. While a certain degree of sacrifice is necessary, there is a line beyond which it becomes unhealthy. Maybe these people haven't fully accepted these parts of themselves. Or maybe they lack the confidence that these parts have an integral role to play in the relationship; they see weeds and not wheat. The "short longer way"[7] is to give these aspects up in order to fit in or try to harmonize but it is a false shortcut, as it leads to far more work in the long run.

This dynamic often comes up when one partner is more religious than the other. The path of least resistance is to avoid the need to integrate the disparate religious aspirations into the home. It takes great courage from both people to see this tension as being a plus, not a minus. Couples that make room for it are enriched with a wider menu of experiences and encounters.

WHAT HAPPENS WHEN TWO PEOPLE ARE able to balance the *me* and *we* in their relationship space? Reese's Peanut Butter Cups. Until 1928, no one ever dreamed that peanut butter covered with chocolate could produce one of the best selling candies of all time. We've got to be able hold on to the essential ingredients of who we are while also blending and joining forces. It could be a huge hit!

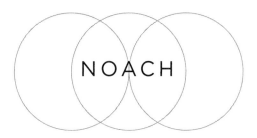

NOACH

Genesis 6:9-11:32

G-d decides to destroy the world and start over,
seeing as human beings have become corrupt, along
with the animals. G-d chooses Noach and his family
as the ones who will populate the new world. Along
with two of every non-kosher animal and seven of
every kosher animal, Noach and his family board the
Ark he built. They live there for almost half a year as
the world around them is destroyed. After the waters
have subsided, they leave the Ark and set out
to build and populate the world.

THE OTHER

THERE IS A SPIRITUAL HANDICAP THAT plagues many couples. Selfishness is not the right word, as it implies awareness of another while prioritizing one's own needs. Self-absorption is closer to the point—focused only on one's self, unaware of others. The only way self-absorption can work (or seem to work) in a marriage is if the other person is willing to play the slave, ensconced in total devotion and surrender.

Maybe your grandparents played this out—Bubbie was the martyr, burning the midnight lamp to serve her husband, children, and grandchildren. Zayde played his part by enjoying the service. He rarely thanked her. Most of us would agree that, while this dynamic was accepted in previous generations, it is not a good model of marriage. My wife and I have a different vision of partnership, one that is based in mutual honoring and empowerment, listening and really hearing, both of us getting our true needs met. But our marriage probably looks more like Bubbie and Zayde's than we want to admit—generosity that all too frequently flows one way, from Ketriellah to me.

Let me illustrate with a personal story I am not so proud of. My future wife and I started dating in the fall. When Hanukkah came, we exchanged gifts. I gave my wife a priceless artifact—my Star Wars C-3PO Pez dispenser. I was shocked that she didn't appreciate it. Granted, the beautiful hand-made bowl and (very practical) gloves she gave me were amazing presents, but how could she not see the value of my C-3PO Pez dispenser!? Thank G-d she helped me understand that, though such a prize might well be invaluable in my world, it was a mere trinket in hers. And if I wanted to give her a gift, I'd have to tune in to what *she* wanted.

Giving is hard. To do it properly, we have to look closely at the receiver's world, letting go of our own fixation on what we value. When we are stumped as to what our partner needs or wants, the block tends to be related to our attention and perception, not our creativity. Once we *see* our partner, the answer will come easily. Did Zayde ever really see Bubbie?

THE FLOOD

The Flood Saga offers clues about how to see—and what to look for. The story starts when "G-d saw that man's evil was abundant upon the earth, and that the thoughts in the hearts of men were only bad, throughout the day." That evil surfaced as theft, cross-breeding,[1] and idolatry,[2] but as Avivah Gottlieb Zornberg writes, their lack of sexual, religious, and moral boundaries all emanated from "a fantasy in which self swells to fill all worlds, a colonial expansionism that radically denies the existence of other worlds of self or culture."[3] People could not recognize or respect the importance—or even existence—of others. Zornberg invokes George Eliot: The

Flood Generation had not yet realized "that the world is not an udder to feed our supreme selves."[4]

The Flood Generation's self-absorption is a stage we all go through—it is humanity's adolescence.[5] The teen years are inevitable and challenging. And they are meant to end right around year 20. Most likely, though, the fantasy that the world is here to satisfy us lingers for far too long, often well into marriage. The "love" that gets us to the *chuppah* is an immature fantasy that our needs will be taken care of—emotionally, psychologically, physically, ethically, financially, religiously. It may sound cynical, but it seems to me that many of us believe (perhaps unconsciously) that our partner is here to keep us company, satisfy us sexually, help raise our kids, and support us in our endeavors—and then leave us alone when we wish. Once we find our way into an agreeable relationship, we continue to invest only as long as it serves this fantasy and doesn't overly challenge our self-centered outlook. Even couples that have been married for decades still struggle to admit the "existence of other worlds." Maybe that's why marriage counselor David Schnarch scoffs at the possibility of "love before marriage."

But let's not be too hard on ourselves. Marriage is usually the first relationship in which we are responsible to an equal. Intimacy is unfamiliar in a lifetime of self-absorption, and that focus is not easily shifted. It takes determination and practice to open ourselves to the demands—and joys—of true relationship. But the opportunity to become a better a person and to truly love another is worth it.

THE LABORATORY OF KINDNESS

In Zornberg's understanding, Noach was not beyond his generation's great illusion. He, too, was unable to absorb the reality of other selves. When G-d told Noach to build an Ark to survive the flood, it did not occur to him to pray for the rest of his generation, as it later would to Avraham[6] and Moshe.[7] But Noach had potential. And for this he was chosen as the progenitor of Human Race 2.0. "And Noach found favor in G-d's eyes."[8]

His classroom would be the Ark—Zornberg calls it a "laboratory of kindness." The curriculum: care for the animals. And care he did. The animals were fed precisely the foods they were used to, and at the exact time that they were used to eating it. In fact, "For twelve months he had not a wink of sleep, neither by day nor by night, for he was occupied in feeding the creatures that were with him."[9] Focusing on the animals trained Noach to tune into an "other," intuit its needs, and satisfy those needs without recompense. After a full year, his brain was successfully rewired toward other-awareness.

Relating, which means perceiving and accepting each other as separate, unique, and worthy, would be the currency of the postdiluvian world—quite a leap from seeing it all as an "udder to feed our supreme selves."

CONSTRUCTING THE LABORATORY

To straighten a bent stick, Jewish wisdom tells us to bend it in the other direction.[10] In order to restore depth to someone we've flattened with our perception, we'll need to exaggerate our focus on them, like Noach did. The laboratory of kindness is the method. Here's how it looks: For a period of time each day, fill your mind and your senses with your partner's needs. Whether for 15 minutes or an hour, be entirely partner-absorbed. Find out—or figure out—what's needed, and be quick on your feet to make it happen. Do it with flare. If you find yourself falling into self-absorption, snap out of it.

In the lab, your brain is being rewired. You will *feel* what makes your lover happy. You will feel the pleasure of delivering that joy. You will experience *da'at*—awareness-in-relationship. And once you taste *da'at*, you will seek more of it. Then the laboratory of kindness will no longer be necessary.

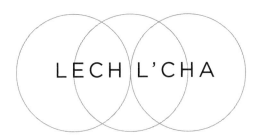

LECH L'CHA

Genesis 12:1-17:27

Avram and his wife Sarai, along with his nephew Lot, cross
into the land of Canaan. Upon arriving, there is a famine,
and they are forced to descend to Egypt. Avram has Sarai
say that she is his sister, so they will not kill him. She is
taken to Pharaoh's harem, but G-d plagues Pharaoh's house,
and she is freed. They leave Egypt very wealthy. Lot is also
very wealthy coming out of Egypt. Avram and Lot have to
part ways, as there is not enough land to feed both of their
flocks. Lot moves to Sodom, where he is kidnapped in the
midst of a war between opposing kings. Avram successfully
fights to rescue Lot. Since Sarai has failed to bear Avram a
child, she gives him her handmaid, Hagar, as a wife. Hagar
conceives and bears a son, Ishmael. Then G-d tells Avram
to circumcise himself and all the males of his household.
After Avram does so, his name is changed to Avraham, and
his wife's name is changed to Sarah. It is traditional to refer
to them by these names, even when referring to the period
of time before their name was changed.

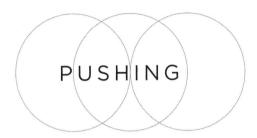

PUSHING

BEFORE I GOT MARRIED, WHILE STILL in the paradise of *yeshiva*, I was free to indulge in my moods and deal with them (or not) as I wished. You might have found me grumpy and distracted for days on end. But when Ketriellah and I tied the knot and broke the glass, my self-absorption was no longer tenable. Our moods swirled around our 500-square-foot home, bouncing off of each other and gathering momentum in the absence of an escape hatch. So, with our limited skills and blunt tools, we tried to connect as best as we could.

What do you without good tools? You compensate with *push*.

Push is scary. We are taught not to do it and to avoid people who do. We are supposed to be suspicious of people who cross boundaries—strangers, door-to-door salesmen, missionaries, people petitioning or raising money for a cause.

Marriage has to be seen differently. The boundaries must be porous enough to allow for a flow of love and concern in both directions, even if imperfectly expressed. This is how the bond is formed and fed. We can have a limited, polite, proper interaction with a mail carrier or a coworker. But marriage is defined in part by two people crossing each other's threshold.

TO LEARN ABOUT PUSH, WE CAN look to Avraham. He built on Noach's work of opening toward others. What Noach struggled for, Avraham expressed naturally and enthusiastically. He was so aware of and devoted to other people's needs that he often neglected his own. Just three days after his circumcision, he was "sitting at the opening of the tent,"[1] looking for passers-by to welcome into his house.[2] Maybe he came off like a door-to-door salesman. But he was quite a salesman—Rashi tells us about the many souls that Avraham and Sarah converted along the way.[3] How did he get past people's fears and suspicions?

AVRAHAM – NO MORE MR. NICE GUY

Avraham is called an *ish chesed*, usually translated as a "kind man." Let's look at his track record. Yes, he welcomes in some guests and spares no expense in caring for them, but he also abandons his father to die in Haran (11:32), leaves his wife in the danger of Pharaoh's harem (12:15), dumps his nephew (13:9), marries his wife's handmaiden (16:4), and then throws her and their son out of his house (21:14). This is kindness?

Clearly, "kindness" is a mistranslation of *chesed*. Some Chassidic masters[4] instead saw *chesed* as synonymous with *hitpashtut*—crossing boundaries, defying internally or externally imposed containment, pushing through both real and perceived limitations in order to make contact. In fact, *chesed* can mean the same thing in the negative: "Any man who takes his sister, either his father's daughter or his mother's daughter, and sees her nakedness and she sees his— it is *chesed*."[5]

In this light, Avraham—the *ish chesed*—lives a life characterized by crossing boundaries into awkward, challenging, or even dangerous situations. He pushes into Canaan, into Pharaoh's house, into a hard conversation with his nephew Lot, and into the lives of strangers.

Avraham is perhaps best known for his roadside inn[6] where he would welcome guests and, over a meal, teach them about the One G-d.[7] Every time he opened a conversation about this very personal subject, he was pushing. Where did he get the courage, the *chutzpah*, to do that? Perhaps his strength was in his disregard for the cultural obsession with being "nice" and "considerate."

IS "NICE" THE HIGHEST PRIORITY?

If one of us is in a bad mood and doesn't want to talk about it, what's the other to do? Many of us wait for an invitation that may never come. Our reluctance to push is understandable, as most of us want to be respectful. We tell ourselves, "If he wants to talk, he'll say so." Moreover, pushy can be mistaken for being nosy or intrusive. But that's not what I'm talking about here, and it's not what Avraham modeled for us. Avraham was willing to push through habitual boundaries for a greater purpose—"And Avraham saw them, and he ran to greet them, and he bowed. And he said, 'Please, my master, if I have found favor in your eyes, please don't go away from me.'"[8] Avraham was pushy, and he is the patriarch of our people. If we want our relationships to be more authentic, alive, and growthful, then it's high time to reevaluate our relationship to "pushy."

I often hear complaints from one partner that the other is not being "nice." This can certainly be cause for concern—kindness is an essential factor in building and maintaining strong, nourishing relationships. But it's not the highest priority all the time. Sometimes the highest priority is to cross the divide between us and forge real, positive connection despite challenges, awkwardness, and resistance. *Chesed* means being present, close, and available. In such moments, the deeper kindness—what some call being "ruthlessly loving"— may not look "nice."

Someone in a bad mood will often send mixed messages, alternately pushing people away and begging for attention. Only a special friend can sort through the contradictory signals and get close enough to offer the love that is so sorely needed. Along the way, the friend actively defies the strong message to "go away" and "leave me alone." Is that person being "nice?"

CHESED VS. BOUNDARIES

There is certainly a time to think about limits and boundaries. We will need to balance line-crossing *chesed* with proper respect for boundaries and distinctions, which is called *gevurah*. Too often, though, we prematurely mix them together. We focus on being nice and polite before chesed is sufficiently developed.

When the reckless enthusiasm of chesed and the boundaries of *gevurah* are mixed before either trait has developed to maturity, the result is dilution, not balance. What we need is a potent mixture of complementary forces. Take the common analogy for *chesed* and *gevurah*—water and fire. Mixing fire with water makes smoke, and then nothing. But setting water in a pot over fire yields many possibilities.

At the beginning of a relationship, or when we decide to make changes within one that's grown stale, it's healthy to cultivate the impulse to be involved in each other's lives. "I want more of you! I want you to have more of me!"[9] There will be plenty of time to learn how to express and receive it properly. But for now, be lovestruck!

It's smart to celebrate our partner's *chesed* toward us, even if it is sometimes unskillful or intrusive, as it is a clear expression of a desire for connection. We can appreciate the *amount* of caring and attention that is being given, even as we help our partner refine its expression.

CULTIVATING *CHESED*

Cultivating *chesed* begins with indulging in what attracts us to each other. With curiosity, courage, and passion, we build our connection around those essential points. We are the building blocks of the relationship, not what we do or how we do it. We are what we give to each other and what we want from each other. I want to give to you. I want to receive from you. Later on we'll figure out what to give and how best to do it.

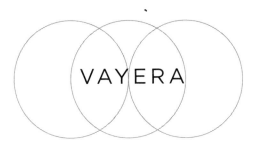

VAYERA

Genesis 18:1-22:24

Having circumcised himself, Avraham sits by the
opening of his tent, ostensibly looking for guests.
Three angels, appearing as men, arrive to give him
the news that Sarah will have a baby within the year.
Sodom is destroyed, and Lot and his daughters are
saved. Sarah gives birth to Yitzhak. As Yitzhak grows
up, Sarah tells Avraham to send Ishmael away, as he
is a bad influence. Avraham reluctantly sends Ishmael
away, along with his mother, Hagar. G-d tells Avraham
to bring Yitzhak as a sacrifice. Avraham takes him to
the top of a mountain and is about to sacrifice him
when G-d stops him. He offers a ram in Yitzhak's place.

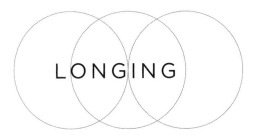

LONGING

MY WIFE AND I ONCE FOUND ourselves tangled in a knot, with each of us tightening it by holding firm to our position. I wasn't getting the love and affection I wanted, and it was bringing me down. Ketriellah insisted that I shouldn't need her affirmation in order to be happy and confident. I was trying to pull love out of her. She was trying to pull self-confidence out of me. It seemed impossible to resolve. I didn't think I could be confident without her affirmation. She didn't think she could affirm me until I showed self-confidence. We were each pushing for what we thought we needed, but the knot only got tighter. Our combined refusal to give in created a level of friction that was almost unbearable. And then it happened. In a moment of pristine clarity, I suddenly realized that I could be confident without her support, and she realized she could drop her agenda around my self-confidence and simply praise me when she wants to. We had thought this shift to be impossible. How wonderful to be wrong!

I have experienced miracles in my life, but this wasn't one of them. On the contrary, this transformation was a direct, natural, predictable result of longing.

AT THE OPENING OF THE TENT

Longing is at the heart of every good story, including Avraham's, which we pick up three days after his self-circumcision (ouch!). The beginning of the *parsha* finds him "sitting at the opening of the tent in the heat of the day."[1] In this one line, Rebbe Natan of Breslov hears volumes. The opening of the tent is "the particular transformation one must go through in order to reach a higher spiritual level." But when a person approaches the opening, "the negative forces rise up against him very intensely." That's the heat of the day. It was Avraham's stubborn willingness to "sit and persist" by the opening of the tent "for many days" that earned him the revelation that followed: "And G-d appeared to him." There have been "many who were close to the opening but turned back."[2]

Rebbe Natan is spelling out a spiritual formula. The call to a higher state (opening of the tent) is followed by a challenge that calls for persistence (sitting) in the face of substantial resistance (heat of the day) and offers a valuable reward at the end (revelation). The formula applies to everyone—spiritual seekers struggling toward refinement, communities aspiring toward unity, couples sensing the possibility of being closer. All are at the opening of the tent. It takes persistence. There will be resistance. The finale is revelatory.

It's no wonder that many people give up. The "heat of the day" pushes us right up to our edge, testing our nerves, patience, and commitment. In its grasp, couples feel like they are fighting instead of growing, like they are strangers living in the same house. They begin to doubt what got them there. Their minds start spinning with questions. Do they really love each other? Is this goal worth all the effort? Is the relationship really worth all this damn struggle?

Rebbe Natan assures us that the "heat of the day" is to be expected and that, yes, the goal is well worth the struggle to get there. But we cannot get there without finding a reservoir of strength.

DO YOU REALLY WANT IT?

How will we avoid being yet another couple that gets "close to the opening but turns back?" It is not a set of skills that is needed here. And it is not a piece of information or a miracle. It is nothing we can gain from the outside. No, in order to break through, we need longing.[3]

So we need to gauge our longing before we strategize about our methods: Is it really important to me to express caring more sincerely? To be more intimate, more honest, more loving? Do I want it so much that I am willing to be more vulnerable in order to get it? Or am I truly satisfied with the way things are?

"Of course I want it," you say. But your initial answer is irrelevant. The truth lies in your kishkes, beyond what you think you want, in how much yearning there really is. If there is enough sincerity, devotion, and commitment, your efforts will bear fruit. If not, you will ultimately turn back, and the "heat of the day" will cool down as the opportunity for change fades away.

Don't know how much longing you've actually got? Don't worry. G-d helps us inventory our longing by putting obstacles in our way.[4] If we quickly turn back, then we know that we didn't really want it—"I'm sorry about canceling our date tonight, but I had to take that meeting." On the other hand, if we forge ahead, leaping over any potential speed bump, then we can know we'll surely get there, and with more resolve than ever—"I told my boss he'd have to reschedule or meet without me. No way am I canceling our night out!"

LONGING TO RESOLVE

A good fight, a conflict full of emotion and intensity, can feel like the "heat of the day" but if you look closer, you'll see that it's really "the opening of the tent." The trick is not to look for a compromise or solution when we are feeling judgment, frustration, or doubt. If we give in, if we succumb to the desire for a return to mere comfort by trying to solve the so-called problem, we end up approaching it as if it were math, while the solution lies in the kishkes. It's longing. That's what broke the stalemate between G-d and Avraham.

The story of the Binding of Yitzhak boils down to a disagreement. G-d wanted him to be sacrificed, and Avraham wanted him to stay alive. Rather than negotiate a compromise as he did when G-d threatened to destroy Sodom[5], Avraham understood that G-d was testing his resolve to do G-d's will.[6] Avraham also wanted to know the extent of his own devotion, so much so that he "woke up early in the morning and saddled his own donkey."[7]

We should remember Avraham when our relationship reaches a crossroads—Dave wants to have another child, while Sarah wants to adopt. Scott wants a new house; Jane wants to live in a yurt. Paula wants more time together, and Jack wants more time apart. It seems like only one (or neither) of us can be happy with the decision we must make. With no hope of resolution, we may be tempted to compromise, give in, or give up.

Instead of seeing conflict as an unsolvable problem, we can learn to hear it as an invitation: Where there is "heat of the day," an "opening of the tent" must be close by, and longing is called for. We should take stock of our longing rather than look for solutions: How strong is our desire to work it out? Or are we looking for an excuse to check out or call it quits? If there is enough longing there, we'll find the right solution.

Avraham's longing was enough to get him past very serious obstacles, both internal and external.[8] As he stood, knife in hand, with Yitzhak bound before him, it was clear that his devotion was paramount: "Don't send forth your hand against the lad, and do not cause him any harm. Now I know that you truly revere G-d, and you did not withhold your precious son from Me."[9]

We may have to get to the sacrificial altar, fully prepared to cast our attachments into the fire of longing, before we see beyond the simple opposites of pregnancy or adoption, house or yurt, more time together or less time together. Our willingness to sacrifice—to willingly give up something important to gain something of higher value—expresses our longing to make the relationship work.[10] With enough longing, the heat of the day will give way and the answer will be obvious.

THREE GIANTS

In Rebbe Nachman's story, The Lost Princess, a king gets angry at his daughter and wishes that the "no-good" would take her, which it does. No one is able to find her the next morning. The *sheni lamelech* (literally, second to the king) searches for her and, at last, finds her captive in a castle. She gives him instructions on how to free her, but he fails twice to follow them. The second time, he falls asleep for 70 years. She leaves a message beside his sleeping body to seek her in the palace of pearls on the mountain of gold. The *sheni lamelech* sets out to look for the palace in the desert and comes across a giant holding a huge tree. He tells the giant about his quest, and the giant tries to turn him back, telling him that he has been fooled, that there is no such place. The giant even calls every animal in the world, each of whom testifies that there is no palace of pearls on a mountain of gold.

The *sheni lamelech*, however, will not be convinced. He insists that such a place exists. Impressed with his perseverance, the giant sends him off to his giant-brother, who is master of all the birds. The same conversation takes place—the giant tries to dissuade him, the birds testify that there is no such place, and the *sheni lamelech* insists on continuing. So the second giant then sends him on to a third giant-brother, who is master of the winds. We then get a third iteration as the giant-master calls all the winds to prove that there is no palace of pearls on a mountain of gold. The *sheni lamelech* still won't budge. Meanwhile, a wind comes late to the meeting. The giant angrily demands, "I called all of the winds. Why are you late?" The wind responds, "I was delayed because I had to bring the princess to the palace of pearls on the mountain of gold."

Rebbe Nachman's story, at its core, is about longing. The *sheni lamelech*'s insistence allows him to get past the giants, who, it should be noted, were very persuasive fellows. According to one explanation, the huge trees they carried represent the enormous amount of knowledge they had.[11] They caused the *sheni lamelech*'s "heat of the day" to boil as they confronted him with compelling reasons to give up. Those giants are the voices, both inside and out, that try to convince us that we cannot succeed. They can make us feel like giving up on happiness, passionate love, intimacy, and freedom. They make the goal seem unreachable. Longing, once again, saves the day. It gets us past them.

The sequence of the story is essential: The princess didn't arrive at the palace until the *sheni lamelech*'s longing reached its peak.

WE MIGHT HAVE A FEW QUESTIONS at this point. What's so great about taking our relationship to the next level? Why does the human soul have such a strong desire to deepen the bond with another? These are big questions with various answers. The most relevant answer for our discussion here is that deep intimacy is the only way to reach areas of our potential that we can scarcely imagine.

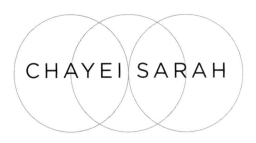

CHAYEI SARAH

Genesis 23:1-25:18

Sarah, Avraham's wife, has died. Avraham purchases a burial plot for her, and then buries her there. Then he sends his servant, Eliezer, to Aram Naharai – where Avraham grew up – to find a wife for his son, Yitzhak. Eliezer goes to the well and develops a plan to find the right woman. He will ask a girl who comes to the well to give him some water, and if she offers to also draw water for his camels, she is the one. Rivkah is the first girl he sees, and she passes the test. He takes her home to become Yitzhak's wife.

HUMILITY

AFTER A FEW YEARS AS A rabbi, I began going over some of my sermons, speeches, and classes with my wife before presenting them to the community. Her feedback has proven to be very valuable, as she brings her unique intelligence and sensitivities to my material. When I then teach the class or give the sermon, I make sure to mention that she helped me develop my thoughts. I want her to know that her contribution affects me and makes a big difference.

It nourishes me so much more, though, when she lets me know how my teachings and writings have affected *her*. When she says, "I was thinking about what you said in your sermon yesterday," I feel powerful and purposeful. And that feels good!

RECALL THAT PROVOCATIVE PHRASE FROM THE first chapter, which the Torah uses to introduce the creation of woman: "It is not good for Adam to be alone. I will make him an *ezer k'negdo*," which loosely translates as "a helper against him." A curious Rabbi Yossi asked Elijah, the prophet, "How, exactly, does a woman help a man?" Elijah answered: "A man brings home wheat. Does he chew wheat? He brings home flax. Can he wear flax? Rather, she enlightens him and stands him on his feet."[1]

In this bibliodrama, the goal is to make food and clothes. To put "food" on the table, two steps are required—first bring the wheat, then make it into bread. To my mind, wheat represents all our raw material, which is really nourishment-in-potential: our ideas, feelings, experiences, talents, dreams, aspirations, drives, fears, flaws, and failings are all on the menu. Anything either partner has ever felt or experienced can bring us closer, can be "food" on our table if we know how to work with it.

It's certainly no forgone conclusion that all wheat will become bread. Intentional refinement is needed. Absent this refinement, unprocessed wheat may become a wedge in the relationship and drive a couple apart. But heaven's the limit for couples who have a steady flow of new material and can turn it into "relationship fodder." All their experiences, even their conflicts, have great potential to provide nourishment. These couples are not afraid to explore, because whatever they find can stoke attraction, passion, and intimacy.

How do you measure up? Answer this one-question quiz: How well do you and your partner get along during and after a visit with one or the other sets of your parents? Family visits tend to bring up tons of emotional material, all of which can be quite useful. Spending time with our family of origin often animates the past, reviving old patterns and familiar, painful feelings. Sometimes we can use these visits as a wonderful opportunity for compassion and patience, both with ourselves and others. At other times, feelings such as shame and helplessness can overwhelm us, quickly regressing us to adolescence or earlier. What tends to happen in your relationship?

MORE THAN HELPING

So you had a family visit, emotions were stirred. Now what? One contribution the bread-maker can make is to help his or her partner approach the raw material at hand. If Kara was triggered by a visit with her mother, Mike can listen to her and ask good questions until she sorts out her feelings. Here, one partner provides what the other partner needs—in this case, clarity about all those feelings that are surfacing.

But good bread-makers don't forget about themselves. One of their reasons for digging, helping, and encouraging is that it brings them benefit too. The first benefit comes when Mike's support helps Kara return to balance in the present moment, which allows her to once again be available to him. The second benefit opens up when the bread-maker turns himself into a student—Mike can now learn from Kara's experience, asking her for support and guidance about how to handle his own family.

THE WATERING HOLE

The urge to nourish both yourself and others is essential to who you are. The ability to fully manifest this urge, however, is usually not. Most of us need help to bring our potential to fruition. Wouldn't it be wonderful if someone cherished your raw material enough to actively participate in its fruition?

Our *parsha* demonstrates the search: When the time came to find a wife for his son Yitzhak, Avraham called upon his servant, Eliezer. Eliezer knew that Yitzhak's raw material would define the future of the Jewish people. And just as Avraham needed Sarah,[2] Yitzhak would need help maximizing the influence of his material. Eliezer's job was to find the right refiner, so when he rolled into the town of Aram Naharaim, he "stationed the camels outside of the city by the *be'er*, the well, towards evening, at the time when the water-drawers would come out."[3]

Why do biblical men (Eliezer, Ya'akov, Moshe) go to the well to find their brides? Because a well is not just a well. Like many Hebrew words, the word for "well", *be'er*, has other meanings as well. Most notably, it implies "explanation." Rav Kook, in the introduction to his commentary on the Talmud, defines *be'er* in the context of Torah learning:

> *There are two ways to go about [contemplating what is contained in the Torah]. The first is to understand what has already been said—to understand all of its implications. This is what we call* peirush—*from the root word PaRaSh, to unfold what is already inside the original source, but is folded up. But there is another way to connect to the original source, based on the enormous potential within a particular passage in the Torah to have implications for* other *related topics and ideas.*
>
> *This power comes not from the original statement itself, but from the Divine Power that invested the world of ideas with the possibility of infinite expansion. From this angle, we approach our original sources with a wide view.*
>
> *And about this process of drawing out new meanings from old sources, it is said, "And it was like a gushing well-spring, a river that never ceases." This is the loftier side of explaining the Torah, and it is fitting to give it the name* bi'ur, *from the word* be'er—"*a well of living waters."* [4]

People find themselves at the well-*be'er* when they need expansion-*bi'ur* of what they have inside but cannot see, do not understand, or cannot actualize. They are looking for a person who can serve as a *be'er* by bringing those deep waters to the surface and putting them to good use.

Eliezer found Rivkah, whose *bi'ur* would refine and expand Yitzhak's greatness. In fact, Rashi tells us, "When the waters saw her, they rose up to greet her."[5] Not only could she refine that material, she could *evoke* it. It would seek her out.

GIVING IS RECEIVING IS GIVING

Finding *bi'ur* is revelatory. Consider a desert where nothing grows until someone channels water into the parched landscape. Suddenly, it springs to life, brown turning to green. We discover a secret when this happens. There must have been seeds there, dry and dormant, waiting for water. But we also learn about the water—see what it can do! Now imagine that same water channeled toward a second desert. It comes to life as did the first, but in its own way: different flowers and trees grow there, different animals come to drink. The water serves both deserts by bringing them to life. And both deserts in turn serve the water as a *bi'ur* by reflecting its potential.

The most satisfying *bi'ur* I can give my partner is to allow her to make my flowers grow. I obviously benefit, but so does she! By allowing her to enrich my life, I let her see her own power. By showing her how much her intelligence, caring, respect and loyalty affect me, she sees a reflection of who she is and what she is capable of.

So when Ketriellah "takes" some of my knowledge and applies it to her life, she is actually giving me the greatest gift, drawing out my power and putting it to good use.

WHAT DO YOU LOVE MOST ABOUT your partner? In what ways do you let this love affect you? What gets in the way of you letting it affect you even more? Do you express gratitude for the gifts your partner brings? What aspects of your partner could you help refine toward their fruition? What might happen if you actively did so? What is stopping you?

OPENING WELLS OF NOURISHMENT CAN BE hard work. And once opened, they can't just be forgotten about. They require diligent maintenance in the face of inevitable entropy. Similarly, when our potentials are awakened, when we see that our life-giving waters are finally being put to good use and our partner's garden starts to respond, we may think our work is finished. A level of powerful relationship has indeed been established. After well-deserved congratulations, though, it's wise to prepare ourselves for a whole new set of challenges, which we will discuss in the next chapter.

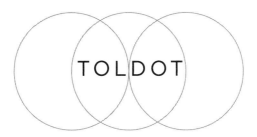

TOLDOT

Genesis 25:19-28:9

Yitzhak moves to the center of the story as his two
sons, Eisav and Ya'akov, are born to his wife, Rivkah.
There is a famine, and Yitzhak heads toward Gerar,
where there is food. He claims that Rivkah is his sister,
but eventually their true relationship is discovered.
He leaves Gerar, but only after becoming quite rich. He
digs out his father's wells, which have been filled in by
the locals out of resentment of his wealth. His servants
then dig a series of new wells, which are claimed by the
locals. Eventually his servants dig an uncontested well.

MAINTENANCE

TEENAGE LOVE IS USUALLY QUITE SUPERFICIAL. Everything seems great until there's an argument. Then the connection dwindles. If only the hurt one could say, "Can we talk? I'm frustrated. It feels like we're growing apart. I need to be able to trust you more." But most teens don't have these communication skills.

We might expect adults, in contrast, to be mature enough to handle conflict, though many of us are not. Moments of confrontation are admittedly risky. If I say I need time apart, he might never come back. If I tell her I need love expressed more strongly, she might cut off the trickle that I'm already getting. If I tell him which shirt I like best on him, he might think I find the other ones ugly.

It's generally true that any move aimed at enhancing connection carries with it some form of rejection or negation. When a woman tells her man that she prefers a heavier massage than the one he is giving her, it may seem that she's rejecting his gift. In actuality, she's trying to fine tune his generosity to maximize its impact on her, though he may not be able to hear it that way. If he could handle her feedback and give her the massage she wants, he would see her genuinely satisfied because of his efforts. That would feel good to both of them. But the ingredient in this stew that sounds like rejection looms large and casts a threatening shadow.

Here's another example: Judy decides to leave work early. She calls her new boyfriend, Joe, and asks him to put on hiking shoes and pack a picnic. They go out for the afternoon together. Her spontaneity, his excitement, and the beautiful spring weather combine to uplift them both, and they share a delightful afternoon together. As the sun sets, he asks her if they could do this every Wednesday. She's put off. She thought it was the spontaneity that made their afternoon so special; scheduling it would take the fun out of it. But he has enjoyed their time together and wants more. She wants appreciation for her great idea and is not ready to think about their next date until she gets it. He is expressing appreciation, but not in a way that makes sense to her. She hears him saying "not enough!" when he is in fact saying "more!"

Good news: They both have a point. They have the chance here to establish a wonderful routine. On the other hand, over-planning might suck the joy right out of it. They both want the same thing, and it's within their reach. But their differing ways of trying to get it are actually pushing it farther away.

IN THE LAST CHAPTER, WE TALKED about water in the desert. We can use that metaphor to see that inspiration or a good intention is not enough. The next step is to put it good use. Finding unexpected water in the dry wilderness is indeed a blessing, but it's just the beginning. It has to be channeled. Obstacles must be removed so the water can flow freely. And it needs to be used smartly. Plants require a specific amount—too little and they dry up, too much and they drown. There are also proper times to plant and to harvest. Weeds too must receive attention—they have to be pulled out so they don't crowd out the plants. The whole endeavor requires specific knowledge, skills, and tools.

Similarly, we contain bottomless wells of nourishment-in-potential—all that material we've been talking about. But discovering a source of nourishment is not enough. We'll have to keep it flowing, unobstructed and well-directed. A healthy flow of nourishment, just as with water, has parameters—we don't want the source to dry up or burn out. What's needed is familiarity with the landscape of the relationship—its seasons and rhythms, its desired fruits and stubborn weeds. All this calls for a set of skills different from those initially required to open the well—skills which Joe and Judy could have used.

Establishing the well was Avraham's *chesed*—digging and pushing until connection is established. After this initial stage, though, continued aggressive outreach will do more harm than good. For the next skill set, we'll sit in the classroom of his son, Yitzhak, who pioneers a whole other kind of love.

LIKE FATHER LIKE SON?

A cursory glance at Yitzhak's biography reveals that he is no Avraham. Avraham was active, Yitzhak was passive. Avraham bound his son to the altar; 37-year-old[1] Yitzhak's role was to not fight it. Avraham actively sent his servant to find a wife for Yitzhak; Yitzhak waited at home.[2] Avraham was a hands-on father, while Yitzhak was not involved with his sons until late in his life. Even then, he certainly didn't bind them on an altar or find a wife for them.

There are other remarkable differences: Avraham refused to choose a favorite son (17:18), while Yitzhak abruptly chose Eisav as his favorite (25:28). Yitzhak didn't fight in any wars like his father did. He never had a hard conversation with a disruptive family member, despite the obvious need to rebuke Eisav for marrying outside of the tribe (26:34). Unlike his father, Yitzhak never argued with G-d or threw anyone out of his house. He also never welcomed anyone *in*, at least without a fight (26:26-27).

Avraham's tent was open on all four sides in order to welcome guests. R' Simcha Bunim adds an epilogue: When Yitzhak took over from his father, he went straight to the hardware store and bought tent pegs to close up all four entrances. Then he sat in his tent and learned with great intensity.[3]

LIKE FATHER LIKE SON!

Despite appearances to the contrary, Avraham and Yitzhak were not opposites. At certain points, Yitzhak acted exactly as his father did. When famine forced him to go to Avimelech King of Gerar (26:7), Yitzhak avoided danger by claiming his wife Rivkah was really his sister, mimicking Avraham's move.[4] And consider the following:

> And all of the wells that his father's servants dug up in the days of Avraham, the Philistines clogged up and filled with dust... And Yitzhak went and re-opened the wells of water that were originally dug in the days of Avraham that the Philistines had stopped up after Avraham had died. And he called them by the names that his father had called them.[5]

As in many parent-child relationships, Yitzhak seems identical to Avraham in some essential ways and opposite in others. But a closer look reveals that their differences lie in method, not intent. Even the classic mystical distinction between them[6]—Avraham-*chesed*-expanding-connecting-traversing, and Yitzhak-*gevurah*-restraint-boundaries-discernment—is describing a chronological development rather than an inherent polarity. The Talmud[7] clarifies: Avraham instituted *shacharit*, the morning prayer, the beginning of the day and setting the day's goals. Yitzhak was the first to pray the *minchah* prayer in the afternoon, sustaining the morning's goals as the day wears on. Both contributions are essential: Avraham creates, Yitzhak maintains. Avraham digs wells, Yitzhak keeps them open. Avraham *names* wells. Yitzhak *upholds* those names—"And he called them by the names that his father called them."

The difference between "naming" and "upholding" is the difference between planting a tree and watering it. Both acts promote the tree's growth, but they are different ways of expressing that intention, just as with Judy's picnic inspiration and Joe's desire to keep it going.

THE MOTIVE

Gevurah skills are absolutely necessary to keep a relationship alive. But restraint and discipline must not lie at the *heart* of the relationship. They *serve* the relationship, but do not *define* it, just as Yitzhak serves his father's legacy but doesn't try to redefine it. Yitzhak understands his mission clearly. He knows he must apply his unique skills toward achieving his father's goals. His motive is his father's motive.[8] G-d even tells Yitzhak that it is Avraham's legacy that matters most: "I will bless you and increase your descendents because of Avraham my servant."[9]

The irony is that, to honor Avraham's legacy, Yitzhak must act in ways that his father could not or would not. You can see why the local Philistines accused Yitzhak of rejecting Avraham's legacy—his actions seemed diametrically opposed to Avraham's.[10]

THE METHOD

The styles of Avraham and Yitzhak are each appropriate depending on the situations at hand. Are we experiencing a lack of water, or are we wasting the water we already have access to? The strategies are opposite: In the first case, we need to dig new wells, cut across boundaries, make something happen; we need Avraham. If we already have a source of nourishment, inspiration, passion, and growth, but for some reason we are not putting it to good use, then we need the skills that will get it flowing and then sustain that flow; we need Yitzhak.

Notice that Yitzhak-work is focused on keeping channels open by removing the debris that clogs them. So while Avraham dealt with water, Yitzhak essentially deals with dirt. Avraham focused on connection, while Yitzhak attends to obstructions.

The potential pitfall is that Yitzhak's love doesn't necessarily feel like love. Many people have a hard time expressing and hearing love when it's clothed in discipline and restraint. But deep relationship requires that we sometimes act in ways that don't seem overtly loving, as we discussed in Chapter 3 while looking at Avraham's pushiness. Some actions are neutral—planning, following through, staying focused, being consistent. And some seem more sharply antithetical to love, like saying no, withholding expressions of love, and taking time apart. If we can't hear or express caring across this whole spectrum, our relationship will stay shallow.

The examples at the beginning of the chapter—those moments of confrontation—deal with the challenge of helping love to expand. The woman who asks for a deeper massage is expressing Yitzhak-love.

When Joe told his wife he wanted to have a picnic lunch every week, he was using Yitzhak-love. When two teens cannot navigate their problems, it is a lack of Yitzhak-love.

Gevurah's discipline, fortitude, precision, focus, practicality, long-term thinking, and dedication can stretch the waters of soul so much farther than *chesed* alone. A relationship that has wells *and* the willingness and know-how to keep them open will forever be like the "garden of G-d."[11]

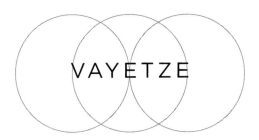

VAYETZE

Genesis 28:10-32:2

*Ya'akov runs away from Be'er Sheva, where his
brother Eisav has threatened to kill him for stealing
their father's blessing. Along the way, he stops at a
nameless place because the sun has set. He gathers
some stones as a makeshift shelter and goes to
sleep. He dreams of a ladder, with angels ascending
and descending. G-d is at the top of the ladder, and
promises He will protect him along the way. Ya'akov
wakes the next morning and consecrates the place.
He goes on his way toward Haran, where he will
ultimately start a family and become wealthy.*

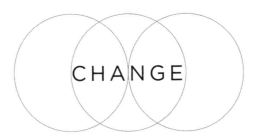

CHANGE

EVEN WITH GOOD TOOLS, IMPROVING A marriage is often not easy. People are complicated—people in relationship, even more so. Just when we have established new, healthy habits, old ones stubbornly rear their heads. Progress is often followed by relapse, which can make us feel like we've accomplished nothing. A day spent in genuine connection could be followed by a week spent in childish quarreling. But we can come to expect the relapse and see it as an important part of the natural pattern that weaves throughout a good relationship.

HARMONY AND COMFORT ARE WONDERFUL, BUT they can be a trap. If we are to grow, we must at some point move toward the next horizon. There are many promising destinations—honesty, cooperation, clear communication, intimacy—and many journeys that take us to them. I've touched on a few of these journeys in previous chapters—moving from self-absorption to awareness of other, and then onto contact, deep connection, and healthy maintenance. Each of the legs of this journey presents unique challenges, but they have much in common, as they are each part of the great journey of relationship.

The Torah speaks of journeys: Adam and Eve's exile from Eden; Cain's aimless wandering; Avraham's forays into and out of Canaan; Yitzhak's trek to Gerar and back; Eliezer's journey to Padan Aram to find a wife for Yitzhak; Yosef's descent to Egypt; Ya'akov's descent to join him there. But none is described in more detail than Ya'akov's trek from his home in Be'er Sheva to his destiny in Haran. Make sure you pack the insights gained from Ya'akov's journey in your own quest for the next horizon.

LEAVING COMFORT...

Stepping away from comfort is the beginning of The Journey. Ya'akov's sojourn starts when he leaves a place called *Be'er Sheva*, "the well of satisfaction," a place of familial and familiar nourishment. His life there was good, saturated with his parents' guidance and love and the sanctity of the Promised Land. But circumstance told him he could not stay, so he courageously left satisfaction in pursuit of destiny. "And Ya'akov left *Be'er Sheva*."

At a certain point, when good enough is no longer good enough, we need to leave *Be'er Sheva*—leave the routines and thought patterns that no longer nourish, or even leave the relationship itself if necessary. But so many people, despite their hunger, stay right where they are. Why? Because they have taught themselves to be satisfied without getting what they truly want. Maybe they think they don't deserve better. Maybe they are afraid to lose everything. So rather than step toward the horizon, they lower their standards to match their reality.

That Ya'akov's brother was trying to kill him for stealing their father's blessing gave Ya'akov an extra push out the door. Most of us are not so "fortunate." Our stalkers are much less dramatic. Typically, they appear as boredom, resignation, apathy, or disconnection. They hardly seem dangerous at all—and are therefore easy to overlook. But it's truly unfortunate not to feel threatened by them, for they are a clear indication of a life headed off track, a wake-up call that we have abandoned our standards. Our soul's survival hinges on seeing them for what they are.

Acknowledging that we want more is the first step away from a life that would lull us to sleep. But the *kavannah* (inner intention) of stepping away is very important. We have to be clear about what we are stepping away *from*. We are leaving the old pattern, not each other. We are leaving a situation that we co-created. We are leaving our old selves behind as much as we are leaving our partner's old self behind. Ideally, we are leaving it together.

...TOWARD ANGER

When "Ya'akov left *Be'er Sheva*"—the well of satisfaction—"he went toward *Haran*." *Haran* means "anger." Moving away from old patterns stirs up all kinds of emotions. When we take those first baby steps away from *Be'er Sheva* toward a richer life, what awaits us is... disorientation and anxiety. Those old patterns, uninspiring as they were, had their own economy: They gave us a small dose of what we wanted along with a large dose of predictability, which is, in turn, about generating a false sense of control. How will we get on outside of these patterns? We used to pout to get sympathy or withhold sex to gain power or put each other in the doghouse to avoid communicating vulnerably. Now what? Without these tactics, we might feel like hungry babies and react accordingly: anger, tantrums, grief, and manipulation.

When those emotions swell, we might want to go back to Egypt, as the Israelites were tempted to do whenever they hit a speed bump. Or we could see those raging emotions for what they are—new territory to explore, the thrill of the unknown, evidence of our bravery. A rocky road doesn't mean that we shouldn't have left the house. It means we are venturing beyond the old, well-trodden highways.

THE SUN SETS

En route to his destiny, Ya'akov stopped at "The Place" because the sun set prematurely.[1] Rebbe Natan of Breslov equates the setting sun with a lack of clear vision and comprehension.[2] Between plateaus of clarity, we are likely to lose our bearings. But this loss of orientation is a powerful gift when we know how to take advantage of it. The "loss of mind" that is spoken of in Kaballah[3] is the prerequisite for the arrival of "new mind"—an upgrade that enables us to interact with the world more effectively.

An "old mind" looks for specific combinations of factors that constitute "good" and "bad." But these standards will change over time if we allow them to. While a child usually defines "good" as "good for me, no discomfort, and immediately gratifying," an adult appreciates the greater good, better in the long run, even at his or her own expense. As long as we can let go of the "old mind," we can redefine. And redefining is essential to a growing relationship.

Our love has to grow as we grow. Love in high school is indeed a shallow affair and cannot compare to the love we feel when we marry. And love before kids is not like love after kids. But how do these evolutions happen? If you could look back at your state of mind during the periods of transition, you would notice a significant amount of distress, but also mystery, challenge, and hope.

That is the moment being described when Ya'akov's sun sets. The old mind is gone, but the new mind hasn't yet arrived. When we are in that liminal space, we experience the world without a clear way of conceptualizing it. We don't have convenient categories with which to frame our feelings and experiences. It's a bit like being blindfolded—we are challenged to explore and perceive the world anew. Stripped of our mantras and cliches, we express hopes and fears in a very raw way.

NEW EYES TO EXPERIENCE MANY COLORS

Since Ya'akov would be overnighting at "The Place," he "took from the stones of the place and arranged them around his head, and he lied down there." For Rebbe Natan, these stones—one for each of the 12 tribes[4]—echo the 12 stones on the breastplate of the High Priest, which contained all possible colors: "A ruby, a topaz, and an emerald…a turquoise, a sapphire and a diamond… an opal, an agate, and an amethyst…a beryl, an onyx, and a jasper."[5]

The color spectrum has expanded. The new phase of relationship won't be in black and white—love, gratitude, discomfort, and frustration will all show up in a more nuanced way. We will be more capable of seeing our lives in their rich complexity rather than in more simplistic and habitual ways. Such a transition couldn't happen without letting go of the old mind.

NEW WAYS OF EXPRESSING LOVE

"Ya'akov took from among the stones of the place and arranged them around his head, and he lied down there…" Rebbe Natan writes that the word "and he lied down"—*VaYiShKaV*—is actually two words, *V'YeSh* and *KV*. The first part of the word, *v'yesh*, means "and behold there are." The latter part of the word is two Hebrew letters—*kaf* and *vet*. Each Hebrew letter has a numerical value.

Kaf vet equals 22, the number of letters in the Hebrew alphabet: "Behold, there are 22!" That is to say, the 22 Hebrew letters are back! Articulate communication has returned in the wake of subtler perception.[6] When the ground of relationship shifts, it is hard to express what we feel, but at a certain point language returns, and with renewed force. Suddenly, we are more capable than ever of articulating our inner experience.

It may be that *what* we are expressing is not glamorous—perhaps pain, alienation, doubt—but we are expressing it more richly than ever before. Do not be dismayed by the initial content. Instead recognize and appreciate the enhanced capacity to communicate, and know that we will eventually apply those 22 letters to more uplifting sentiments.

To illustrate, here are five ways to express the same reaction:
- (stamping feet and walking out, stage left).
- "You're a jerk!"
- "I'm really angry!"
- "I'm angry that you tried to solve my problems rather than just listen."
- "When you try to solve my problems for me, I feel belittled and not trusted, and then I close up."

THE DREAM OF THE LADDER

Ya'akov slept and dreamed, "and behold! There was a ladder upon the ground, and the top reached up to the heavens. And angels were ascending and descending upon it." It was a vision of what he was already experiencing—ascents and descents marked by rest stops of safety with spaces for risk-taking. After the dream, he realized he could anticipate and articulate the stages of his life journey. And his faith was strengthened that G-d had been and would be with him throughout.

Similarly, relationship presents like a ladder, and many of the steps can be anticipated. When we know roughly what to expect, we will not be thrown by the spaces between the rungs. Instead, we will enjoy them as invitations to reach and to leap.

YA'AKOV WAKES UP

Looking back, Ya'akov realized that his struggles were saturated with G-d's loving-kindness and constant guidance. What he had perceived as a fall from grace – running away from his parents' home, leaving the land of Israel—was in fact an invitation to a higher level of relationship. "And Ya'akov woke from his slumber, and said 'Behold! G-d is in this place, and I did not know!'"

It is certainly easier to notice and celebrate growth after the fact, and it is important to do so! We benefit when we name it, discuss it, and develop a vocabulary for it. Express gratitude for those accomplishments and celebrate them. Compare notes about how things started to fall apart, how scared or frustrated we were, how we weathered the challenges, and how we grew so much from it. Why so important? So that next time the challenges come, as they surely will, we can remind ourselves and each other that this process is normal, healthy, and necessary for the growth of our relationship. We are mapping the terrain of our relationship so that we can be better prepared next time the road beckons.

GO TELL IT ON THE MOUNTAIN

"And Ya'akov picked up his feet, and went off to the land of the people of the East." Rebbe Natan writes that, after Ya'akov's dream, he went on to tell the world about what he'd been through. After all, this is important stuff. The evolution of Ya'akov's relationship to G-d provides essential experiential information that applies to every good relationship. And what we learn through these processes can be very helpful to others. When other couples are struggling and stressed, we can help. We can help them see their crisis as the potential end of one particular chapter of the relationship rather than as a reason to throw the whole thing out the window. And we can tell them about the road ahead, warn them of where the potholes are, and remind them of the joy that awaits them when they reach their destination.

REAL LIFE

Having been through so many cycles of disconnection and reconnection, Ketriellah and I have developed a pretty good sense of the pattern itself. When do we feel more in love? What situations tend to trigger us? What can we do about it?

Each couple has their own way of experiencing the stages of The Journey and will develop their own unique tools for each stage. Here's one that Ketriellah and I use for the "reintroduction of language" phase: At certain points I have found myself mumbling vitriol about some unsatisfying aspect of my life. Ketriellah found the mumbling itself intolerable, and the substance of the mumbling (if she could decipher it) equally difficult to take. For a long time, it caused frustration and fighting. At a certain point, I realized that I wasn't trying to communicate—I was mumbling because I needed to get the words out. I didn't need a response quite yet. Now, when she asks, I can say, "I just need to mumble." Eventually, after the mumble phase, I'll figure out what it is I need to say, and I'll say it in a way that she can hear.

VAYISHLACH

Genesis 32:3–36:43

Ya'akov has left Lavan's house with a full family and enormous wealth. The first thing he does is send messengers to his brother Eisav. He learns that Eisav is coming to meet him, with 400 men in tow. Ya'akov prepares for the encounter, in part by sending him several herds of animals as a gift. After returning to his previous camp to recover some jugs he left there, Ya'akov wrestles with an angel. The angel gives him a new name—Yisrael. The next morning, he encounters Eisav. Eisav reluctantly accepts Ya'akov's gift, and they go their separate ways.

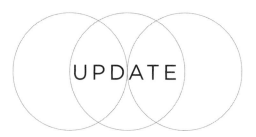

UPDATE

SHIFT HAPPENS

YA'AKOV'S EPIC JOURNEY FROM BE'ER SHEVA to Haran and back took 22 years. Here's how to do it in one day—and why it's important to be able to do so.

Our lives are in a constant process of change as we engage in our various activities—work, raising children, reading books, socializing, listening to the radio, meditating, praying, climbing mountains, or playing music. The continual shifts are often subtle: a small insight while talking to a friend, a new move during a climb, a soft emotional opening during prayer. On occasion, the shift is more like an eruption—a flood of feelings pouring forth during a funeral, a life-changing revelation in a therapy session, a sudden health crisis.

Change, even when measured in milligrams, happens constantly. And our relationship shifts accordingly. Some amount of new material has been put on one side of the delicate scale that keeps our shared lives in balance. The shift has to be acknowledged and integrated, the scale recalibrated.

Every experience of change, no matter its size, points us toward the same road that Ya'akov traveled: disintegration, growth, and reintegration. Sometimes the shift in direction is half a degree; sometimes it feels like a full about-face. But regardless of the magnitude, as soon as one of us says, "This has changed me," we both need to get to work on some level, letting go of the old thinking and developing a new connection in light of the new material.

Or, the other option, the new material can be dismissed, ignored, or buried.

Tragically, too many couples are unable or unwilling to integrate their ongoing, independent experiences into their relationship. Their marriage is roadblocked by the fear that they cannot meet the challenge of change.

When a relationship is not re-calibrated and updated, it cannot meet both partners' needs. A harmful cycle gets set in motion: They shift their attention to other people who can hold the feelings and insights that would surely enrich their marriage, were they to bring them home. A woman shares an accomplishment in climbing with her climbing group but not with her husband; the profound Torah insight is discussed with a learning partner but left out of the marriage; the transformational prayer experience is articulated and honored in the house of prayer, but it's business as usual at home. As those other relationships become richer and more meaningful, it becomes easier and more appealing to talk about our experiences in those other places, and harder to bring them home. The more outdated the relationship gets, the less likely a couple is to bring their important moments to each other. This trajectory of disconnection is fueled when potential moments of shared growth get sacrificed on the altar of the *status quo*.

ADDICTED TO CHANGE

We can overcome this fear of change when we truly experience the benefits of integrating new material. This once-feared process becomes accepted, appreciated, eagerly anticipated. Soon enough, we start actively seeking new material and can't wait to integrate it with each other. Maybe Ya'akov was expressing this enthusiasm when, after 22 years with crooked Lavan, he marched straight toward Eisav, demanding a meeting. The Midrash sounds downright shocked that Ya'akov would send for his brother at this point. "[Eisav] was going on his way and you send him messengers, saying 'thus says Ya'akov!?' This is like one who wakens a sleeping dog!"[1]

Why would someone wake a sleeping dog? Is he a fool? Or maybe he knows that, until he confronts that dog, he will have to live in fear of it.

This is what we are seeing with Ya'akov: After years of orbiting around Yitzhak, Rivkah, Eisav, and Lavan, he has finally learned to steer his own course. Emboldened by his newfound self-direction, he wants to confront the one person who he knows might make him doubt his strength. It's as if his new achievement is not fully *his* until he knows Eisav cannot take it away.

Obviously, our partner is not our enemy like Eisav was to Ya'akov. But confrontation can be scary, nonetheless. And if we can get good at it there, in our most important relationship, we can do it just about anywhere.

THE CHOICE

Marriage and religion contain some of the hardest relationships to keep up to date, perhaps because these arenas demand integrity, awareness, faith, and flexibility. We've all heard the lore of the Jewish PhD who is stuck at a 2nd grade Jewish outlook and wonders why services and rituals are not meaningful to her as an adult. Her Jewish perspective has not been updated, and nothing is forcing her to do so. Marriage, on the other hand, has automatic update mechanisms in place—you cannot go to marriage twice a year like High Holiday services. We see each other all the time, are strongly affected by each other all the time, push each other's buttons all the time. And we encounter many of life's most important moments together. So our choices are limited: we either find a way to make our marriage relevant and up to date, get divorced and try again with someone else, or become a robo-spouse.

Think about the couples you have known—what have they chosen? And do you admire them for it?

HOW TO SHARE VICTORIES

Even when we have realized the necessity of bringing important individual experiences to our marriage, there are many factors to consider in terms of method. For example, where was your partner while you were having that experience? Did you have that cathartic climbing moment while he was watching the kids? Did he have to clean up the messy kitchen while you were finishing your book's triumphant last chapter?

We will have to approach these conversations with good intentions. Does she want to tell him about her moment in the climbing gym in order to raise them both up? That perseverance that got her to the top of the wall—is she willing to bring it to bear in their relationship as well, or does he think she cares about climbing more than their marriage? She might want to ask herself whether she hopes her newfound confidence from climbing will inspire an equally powerful shift in her partner. Does she want to encourage her husband to have thrilling experiences of his own? Would she be willing to rearrange her schedule to make that happen?

On the other side, the listener would benefit from asking: When my partner is trying to bring some of her own accomplishments into the relationship, does my alarm sound? Do I assume it will harm me? Do I resent her for pursuing her dreams when I don't have the guts to pursue mine? Am I disregarding her experience because I feel abandoned when she goes climbing, or is it perhaps because I'm afraid to see her so powerful?

I recall a time when my wife was sharing an amazing breakthrough with me that she'd had that day. I had been checking e-mails and continued to do so while she spoke. Only later did I realize just how powerful her breakthrough had been, and just how applicable it was for me as well. It took me some time to realize how ego-driven my unwillingness to pay attention actually was. I had to ask her to tell me again, after apologizing for not listening the first time.

PRACTICAL STEPS

Consider the following scenario: Jane has just wrestled the kids to bed and is cleaning up from dinner when Sam bursts through the door, fresh off a gig with his band, smiling and carefree. He can't wait to tell his wife about how wildly the crowd responded to his new song. He opens his mouth to tell her and... stop.

Sam! The energy will not fade so fast that you have to tell her right now! Take a breath. Assess the situation. Acknowledge what is happening for Jane. Jump in, and do some dishes, wipe off the table, make the lunches. Later, at the right time, say, "Thanks for putting the kids to bed. I've been dying to tell you about the show."

It is important to create a particular space and time to convey that exciting experience—"How about getting a babysitter tomorrow night so I can catch you up on what I've been going through?" "When would be a good time to show you pictures from my trip to Yellowstone?" Maybe even a weekly meeting: "Can we set up a regular date night on Thursdays so we can catch up on our independent lives?" Preparation puts us both in the proper frame of mind.

YOUR VICTORY IS MY VICTORY

One person's insights and breakthroughs inevitably affect the other. If my partner is carrying new power that hasn't been integrated into our relationship, it's like an invisible weight on our scale. We both feel its presence, but we can't figure out what to adjust. Once that power is understood and successfully integrated into the relationship, we can rearrange ourselves accordingly, and then we can relax. The update to our connection will relieve and nourish us both—the climber's accomplishment raises the bar for both of them.

The goal here is to realize that one partner's great moments are a resource for both of us, and whichever one of us has a new experience has it for *both of us*. This is true on many levels. First, it's great to have someone powerful on your team. Whether this strength manifests in more patience for the kids, a brilliant clarity that can move us through thorny issues, or more fun and joy in the household, it serves us both.

Another benefit: partners often find themselves dealing with similar or parallel issues, stumbling over the same obstacles. Access to each other's mistakes and victories will save us time, energy, and aggravation. When Jane figures out how to get Johnny to eat his oatmeal,

Sam need not reinvent the spoon. But he might have to get over his wounded ego because he didn't figure it out first.

HAVING EVERYTHING

Even more is alluded to in Eisav and Ya'akov's face-to-face dialogue. Ya'akov had sent Eisav a gift, which Eisav tried to refuse, saying, "I have so much. Take what is yours." But Ya'akov insisted, telling him, "But I have *everything*."[2]

The difference between having so much and having everything is infinite. "I have so much" defines someone who lives in the world of quantities. Eisav's is a competitive world of finite stuff and power that only one of us can have at any given time. What you have—joy, energy, clarity—I cannot have. If you're relaxed and happy, then I'm not.

In Ya'akov's world, though, it is possible to have everything. How? By expanding the circle of self to include both of us: If you have it, then I have it, too. I have no particular preference between your power and mine. Your victories *are* my victories, not because they serve me or teach me, but because we are together. In the words of the Talmud, *ishto k'gufo*—his wife is like his own body.[3]

After walking Ya'akov's journey enough times, we won't be fearful of or threatened by change and growth. We will welcome it, whichever of us it comes through.

VAYESHEV

Genesis 37:1–40:23

Ya'akov settles in the land of Canaan, but trouble
comes quickly. Yosef's prophetic dreams in which he
is leading the family threaten to shatter the family's
delicate peace. Under Yehuda's leadership, the brothers
attempt to get rid of Yosef by throwing him in a pit
and then selling him as a slave. Yosef ends up in Egypt,
where he is successful in running his master's house
but is thrown in prison after his master's wife tries
to seduce him. Meanwhile, Yehuda goes off to live a
mundane life, but meets with tragedy as two of his
sons die. He impregnates his daughter-in-law, who
he thinks is a prostitute. She bears twins, the older of
which is Peretz, the ancestor of King David.

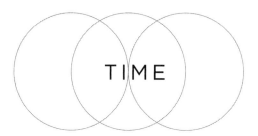

TIME

TIME TO GROW

Even good tools don't work without a healthy relationship to time.

Ya'akov had an understanding of time that confused the people in his life. When his brother Eisav invited him to join forces and quickly dominate the world (33:12 with Rashi), Ya'akov refused, reminding Eisav,

> *My master, [you know] the children are tender, and I am respon-*
> *sible for the sheep. If you push them one day, they will die. You*
> *pass before me, and I will go at the pace of the work I have to do,*
> *and at the pace of the children (33:13-14).*

When his daughter Dinah was raped, Ya'akov's was silent (34:5) and even criticized his over-zealous sons' act of vengeance. They were exasperated by his lack of response: "Shall our sister be treated like a whore?!" And as he watched his sons fall into mutual animosity, he did nothing to facilitate a peaceful resolution.

What held Ya'akov back? He fully knew what many of us struggle to realize: nothing of value can be accomplished before it is ready to happen. Difficult challenges in important relationships cannot be overcome in an instant. Relationships proceed "at the pace of the work that must be done."[1]

Don't despair—Tel Aviv wasn't built in a day. Rather, hear the equation in reverse: *anything worthwhile can be accomplished with enough time.* A story is told of Akiva, an unlearned shepherd, who came to a well to drink. He found himself asking, "Who dug this well?" First, the answer came: "It is the water that drips continually upon it." Then, revelation: "If something soft [like water] can erode something hard [like rock] then surely something hard [like the Torah] can erode something hard [like my heart]." Rather than being discouraged by the time it took for the water to carve the hole, he heard that time can bring powerful changes. That day, starting in the local kindergarten (he was aged 40 at the time), he embarked on a quest that led him to become the premier rabbi of his generation.[2]

Rabbi Akiva and Ya'akov offer an admonition that we usually only pay lip service to: real change takes time. And in the same breath, they encourage us: with time, real change *will* happen. Armed with this information, we gain perspective on our challenges as a couple—this is a lifetime of work. We can't expect a sea change tomorrow or next week. We simply cannot make the process move faster than it can bear. But if we do the work today and tomorrow, we will eventually reach our goal. Anger, impatience, and unrealistic expectations will not make it move any quicker.

When Akiva went to tell his wife Rachel he was going off to learn, she let him go for *12 years*. She certainly understood that growth takes time. Upon his return, he overheard Rachel and a neighbor talking. The friend disparaged Rabbi Akiva for leaving his wife alone for so long. He heard Rachel's reply: "I'd let him go for another 12 years!" Without entering the house, he went back to the academy and learned for another 12 years. When he returned again, he was the undisputed leader of the generation, and he publicly acknowledged his debt to her.[3]

Too many couples don't see their work as a marathon. They invest in short-term solutions for problems like sexual frustration and incompatibility, strained communication, divergent goals, and different approaches to parenting. While some tactics can help in the short term, intelligent persistence over time is the only way to change. And if we persist, we *will* see the change we need.

SLOW BUT NOT STAGNANT

Ya'akov saw no benefit in running ahead to finish the race with Eisav before the world was ready. And there was nothing to gain in chastising Yosef for arrogantly reporting his dreams because Yosef was not yet ready to receive this guidance. But he had another motive for not chastising him. In Yosef's dreams, his brothers bowed down to him, and justifiably so. Yosef exhibited, in raw form, the leadership that would lead to the whole family's evolution. The dreams, therefore, were not only about personal arrogance. So we read that "Yosef's brothers hated him; but his father kept the matter in mind."[4]

Reality check here: Ya'akov's practiced relationship to time should not be reduced to simple patience. Right after demonstrating restraint with Yosef, he started pushing impatiently, sending Yosef off to see to the "peace" of his brothers who were off shepherding near Shechem. What was he thinking? Didn't he know that they hated him and might try to harm him? And what sort of wicked irony did he intend by sending Yosef to see to the "peace" of his brothers?

The answers are wrapped up in Ya'akov's nuanced approach to time. He knew you cannot rush healthy change. But he did not advocate inertia or passivity. Even though he refused Eisav's offer to run ahead to the end of the race, he didn't ignore the challenge—he set out toward that goal, but at his own speed: "I *will* go at the pace of work I have to do and at the pace of the children, and I *will* eventually catch up with you at Se'ir."

Similarly, watching his sons' growing animosity toward each other, Ya'akov saw the danger that the brothers would simply disengage: Yosef would pursue his dreams, the brothers their career as shepherds, and they would greet each other with fake smiles at family reunions and life cycle events. But Ya'akov knew they each had work to do, particularly with each other. And he saw that they needed a little nudge.

DIFFERENT KINDS OF PEOPLE

Brothers can try to run away from each other, but marriage is another story. It gets its strength from our dogged insistence on making it work. Despite our differences, we keep coming back for more. Those very differences provide our hardest challenges. But when the friction of difference transforms into healthy polarity and mutual learning, we become very wealthy.

Our differences, when met with perspective, patience, and perseverance, provide the drops of water that can open our hearts. Each time we navigate the tension of our different approaches we get closer to the goal. Listening when we don't agree has this effect, even if we still don't agree after we've listened. Saying a healthy "no" to an unhealthy behavior is one drop. Refusing to get drawn into a fight is another. Every time we remember our values under stress, cool off after feeling angry, or genuinely forgive, we are carving out more room in our hearts. One at a time, over time, these drops carve the well.

Marriage provides a steady flow of drops for the well; G-d also provides. As the Talmud says, "One who comes to purify himself is helped."[5] Ya'akov understands his role concerning his sons in this way. He won't allow his sons to stray too far from each other, but he also cannot force them to resolve their differences. He trusts G-d will continue where his own reach leaves off by forcing them to face what they need to work on. He sets up a possible confrontation by sending Yosef out to see his brothers. That's as far as he can reach. Ultimately, he believes Yosef will see to the peace of his brothers.

REAL LIFE

Ketriellah and I have not had a single fight that didn't lead to better understanding, more patience, or deeper appreciation. We don't go looking for fights, and we don't enjoy it while it's happening. But we know that, once the dust settles, there will be a bit more room in the house for our fullness.

We're not in a rush. Ketriellah says that she'll come into her own by the age of 50. This view applies to our marriage as well—we're not going to reach our ultimate goal today or tomorrow. But the journey between here and 50 is made up of thousands of todays and tomorrows. And each of them brings us closer.

Remembering this sense of time, we can relax within our mistakes. Our fights might define a frustrating moment, but they do not define our potential. In fact, the opposite: the friction they provide wears away our resistance to each other.

BETWEEN NOW AND THE FUTURE, WE still need to deal with our flaws, just like Yosef and his brothers must do. And here in our ancient story, they are still far from this happily-ever-after. Each of the brothers has yet to confront his own Achilles' heel. And he won't confront it until he gets past the most formidable foe of all: the beast called shame.

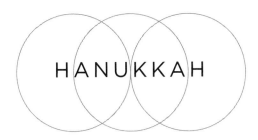

HANUKKAH

Embrace your worst fear.
Become one with the darkness.
— Ducard, in Batman Begins

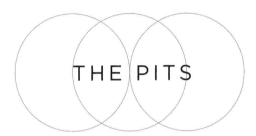

THE PITS

REAL LIFE

I worked with a man who was accused of emotionally abusing his then-wife. As we unraveled the issue, we homed in on his low self-esteem. Being shorter than average, he had always compensated for his small size with a big voice and quick wit. Any challenge to his power was met with a loud and scathing response.

I encouraged him to look at his shame about being short. From an early age, he associated shortness with inferiority and sought to compensate as best he could. Nestled within that association is a sense that it is better to be smarter or more powerful than other people. The obvious shadow here: fear of being weak.

I recommended that he address this fear with the following prompt: "If I weren't afraid of appearing weak, I would..." I figured that his fear of powerlessness was being expressed as blaming others, in partic-ular his wife, who happened to be taller than him. Blaming, like any reactive behavior, distanced him from his vulnerability. It allowed him to keep his fear walled off. I was surprised and happy for him that he was able to respond with curiosity. He said, "Tell me more about that..."

HANUKKAH – SHORT SHRIFT

Every holiday that calls for any kind of ritual observance has a volume of its own in the Talmud—Shabbat, Yom Kippur, Sukkot, Purim. Hanukkah is the exception—it gets only about four pages in the entire Talmud. Three of these pages are nestled in the tractate that deals with Shabbat, specifically in the section that discusses what oils and wicks may be used for Shabbat candles.

The Talmud uses this as a segue to discuss what wicks and oils may be used on Hanukkah and then goes on to relate the famous argument between the sages Hillel and Shammai: Hillel says to light one candle the first night and to add one candle each night. Shammai says to light eight candles on the first night and one less each night until the eighth night gets a single candle. After this discussion, we are given the shortest possible synopsis of the Hanukkah story.[1]

Then the Talmud interrupts its discussion of Hanukkah to call our attention to a strangely phrased verse from the Torah: When Yosef was thrown into a pit by his brothers, "the pit was empty. It had no water in it."[2] The Talmud notes the redundancy: If the pit was empty, isn't it obvious that there was no water in it? The answer is that it was empty of water, but there were snakes and scorpions in there.[3] Then the Talmud returns to its discussion of Hanukkah. Granted, the Yosef story is always read around Hanukkah, but it still seems like strange editing...

HANUKKAH IS THE PITS

... or maybe by inserting its interpretation in that exact spot, the Talmud wants us to think of Hanukkah as a pit. After all, the Hanukkah candles are ideally lit within 10 *tefachim* (hand-breadths) of the ground,[4] a height below which the Divine Presence does not reach.[5]

We always read the Yosef story around Hanukkah-time. And Yosef spent a great deal of time in pits. His brothers introduced him to his first pit when they were infuriated by his dreams.[6] He was pulled out of that pit and sold to a band of Ishmaelites who brought him down to Egypt where he was sold to Potiphar, one of Pharaoh's ministers.[7] When Potiphar's wife tried to seduce him and failed, she turned the story around and accused him of making advances on her. He was once again thrown into a pit—Potiphar's jail.[8] There, he interpreted the dreams of a wine steward and a baker. Having given the wine steward the favorable interpretation that he would once again pour wine for Pharaoh, Yosef asked him to champion his cause. After all, "I was stolen from the land of the Hebrews, and in this place I didn't do anything, and they put me in a pit!" But the wine steward forgot about Yosef entirely.

At this point in the story, Yosef has spent 12 of his 30 years in pits and prisons,[9] and Hashem is willing to leave him there until….until what? My understanding is that he will not be freed until he takes responsibility for what has befallen him. After all, Yosef wasn't as innocent as he claimed to be. In the simple reading of the story, he comes off as a vain, arrogant tattler. The first thing the Torah tells us about Yosef is that he was *na'ar*, which means "youthful."[10] Rashi explains that he was vainly doing "youthful things, like fixing his hair, batting his eyelashes, and making himself beautiful." We are then told—as I discussed in the last chapter—that he reported all his brothers' misdeeds to their father without holding anything back.[11] Further, he showed no sensitivity in relaying his dreams to his brothers: "Listen to this dream I had [where you all bow down to me]."[12] It's no wonder his brothers wanted to be rid of him!

And he was no less responsible for the situation with Potiphar's wife. As Rashi tells us, "When Yosef saw himself ruling [Potiphar's house], he began to eat and drink and curl his hair. G-d said, 'Your father is in mourning, and you are curling your hair?! I will sic the bear [Potiphar's wife] on you!'"[13]

Yosef would have done well to turn that critical moral eye on himself instead of his brothers. But, alas, we see no indication that he was willing to do so. And so his prison sentence stretched on and on. All that power, stuck in potential because Yosef continued to blame others for suppressing it.

THE PIT OF POWERLESSNESS

Power is defined as "the ability to act or produce an effect." Marriage takes power: From cleaning to inspiring, from bringing home a paycheck to overcoming an unhealthy habit, from conveying love to receiving love, we are constantly required to be active and effective. And yet, far too many of us come up far too short.

Marriage provides us with the perfect opportunity to hold someone else responsible for our failures. This one person is always there, always involved in one way or another. We can pin any kind of failure on this ever-present scapegoat, from a boring date to unexciting sex, from being overweight to a thin social life, from a lack of personal integrity to an inability to achieve goals.

This mentality will get us where it got Yosef. It's a sad excuse that says more about who we are than who our partner is. It means we have accepted powerlessness. But the blame itself is the pit. As long as we blame, we are powerless.

Like Yosef, many of us have been blaming others for our lack of power from the start – G-d, fate, parents, society, genetics. While societal oppressions such as sexism and racism do exist, when we lock ourselves into the reactive blame game, we are actually relinquishing any chance to connect to our power. The truth is that, as far as our personal situation goes, we ourselves have dug the pit we live in. There is no one else to blame for our being there and no one else who can get us out.

For 12 years, this inconvenient truth was too scary for Yosef. It was completely at odds with his view of the world and would have required admitting that his victim story was fiction. But as long as he refused to accept that he had dug his own pit, he would not go free. Finally, two years after the wine steward's release, Yosef got it.[14] Writhing in the pain of hard self-discovery, he let out a scream from the depths of his soul. At that exact moment, Pharaoh had his dream. A few hours later, Yosef was running Egypt.

HOW WE TURN THE PIT INTO POWER

We don't know exactly what triggered Yosef's realization, or what will trigger ours. But we'll know we're getting close when we stop seeing the pit as a place to get out of and start seeing it as a place—a sacred Place, actually—to find truth in. When we stop blaming, we'll see how much power suddenly becomes available.

The prison that made us weak has become an access point to hidden power. This is the power that fueled Yosef's ascent and can fuel ours as well.

Recall the snakes and scorpions in Yosef's first pit. These are relatively small creatures, yet their great power makes them universally feared. Our fears—our snakes and scorpions—make us want to get out of the pit rather than stay long enough to discover and absorb the power that's there. When we stick around despite the fear, the pit vanishes. When Yosef finally summoned the courage to confront what he was most afraid of—that he, and only he, was responsible for his failures—he was catapulted to the throne room almost instantaneously. He turned his pit into nourishment, turned *BoR* into *BaR*.

So how do we start seeing our pit as a Place? Hanukkah and Hillel light the way. A significant portion of our success in life and relationship depends on our ability to see what the darkness is trying to hide. The power of Hanukkah is that it provides the lights by which to see under 10 *tefachim*, in the darkness, in the pit. Hanukkah gives us the opportunity and the courage to look at what is frightening us so we can reclaim the power that we have invested in those fears.

How does Hillel help? Hillel adds light every night. Why would someone need more light? Because it's getting darker. Hillel is going deeper and deeper into the pit, because he knows how much power is stored there. The light of Hanukkah allows us to peek beyond fear and find power.

Beyond the snakes and scorpions is a wellspring of not only power, but also freedom and joy. We only need the courage to confront them, and that courage is given to us on Hanukkah, when a small ragtag Jewish army defeated the great legions of Greece. How does it work? That is the miracle of Hanukkah.

THE FRIEND I WAS WORKING WITH was afraid of being rendered powerless. By giving in to those fears, by blaming others for his lack of power, he had actually rendered himself powerless. Hopefully, he'll continue to approach that fear with curiosity and keep looking it in the eye until he uncovers his own power. If he does the work, he will find strength that cannot be taken away.

So now it's your turn, if you want one. What are you afraid of?

MIKETZ

Genesis 41:1-44:17

Pharaoh has a disturbing dream that he knows is
prophetic but cannot interpret. When his advisers fail
to find its meaning, Yosef is summoned from prison, as
he has a reputation as an accurate dream-interpreter.
Yosef knows that Pharaoh has subtly misrepresented
his dream, and he intuits how the dream actually
played out—and the reason for its misrepresentation.
Seeing Yosef's wisdom, Pharaoh makes him the viceroy
of Egypt, placing him in charge of grain distribution.
Meanwhile, as per Yosef's interpretation, Egypt and the
entire region is hit with famine, which brings everyone—
including Yosef's brothers—to Egypt to buy grain. They
do not recognize Yosef, and he uses his disguise to
manipulate them toward confronting their past.

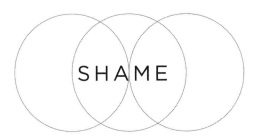

SHAME

PHARAOH HAD A DREAM, A VERY disturbing dream for a Pharaoh to have. He saw himself standing on the River Nile, from which seven healthy cows emerged. Then seven sickly cows came out of the river and swallowed them up.

Pharaoh felt uneasy. He knew the dream was important but wasn't clear on its meaning. And there were other, more logistical reasons why it didn't sit right with him. First, the Nile was a god in the Egyptian pantheon, so standing on it was sacrilegious, even for a Pharaoh. Second, according to ancient Egyptian theology, only good could come out of the Nile, so it was inconceivable that the Nile would produce the seven scrawny cows.[1]

In the Talmudic formula, we dream at night what we think about during the day. Clearly, then, Pharaoh did not accept the hierarchy of the Egyptian pantheon or its rules. By their standards, he aspired to be a higher god than the Nile. His ambition would not be viewed positively by the Egyptian priests. And his claim that the Nile could produce unhealthy cows made him something of a heretic.

Pharaoh was in a bind. He needed an interpretation of his dream but couldn't fully disclose it. "And Pharaoh called to all the wise men of Egypt, and to all the necromancers, and he told them his dream." Surely he told them the same edited version he would eventually tell Yosef: "In my dream, I was standing *on the banks* of the river...And seven other cows came up after them..." (omitting that they came *from* the river).[2] Not surprisingly, "none could interpret it for Pharaoh."

Then the wine steward remembered Yosef, who had accurately interpreted his dream ten years before. Maybe the Hebrew slave could do the same for Pharaoh. Yosef was hurried from the pit and brought before the Egyptian ruler. As Pharaoh told of cows and corn, Yosef knew he was not telling the whole story. And he knew *why*: Pharaoh's deception was motivated by an emotion familiar to Yosef, an emotion that weaves through the entire Egypt story: shame.[3]

YOSEF'S SHADOW

Yosef's mother knew shame. While her sister Leah had already borne four sons to Ya'akov, Rachel was childless. "And Rachel saw that she had not borne children to Ya'akov, and Rachel was jealous of her sister. And she said to Ya'akov, 'Give me sons! For if you don't, I am like a dead woman!'" When at last Yosef was born, his mother Rachel said, "G-d has withdrawn (*asaf* – same root as *Yosef*) my shame." Relieving his mother's shame was Yosef's namesake. But it would be some time before he would deal with his own.

Rachel's shame was linked to her inability to bear children. Yosef's was based on his inability to guide and unite his family. His vision of his family's future evoked resentment rather than harmony: "...and

Yosef dreamed a dream and told it to his brothers, and they increasingly hated him."[4] His powerful moral compass divided the family instead of uniting it: "And Yosef brought reports of their misdeeds to their father Ya'akov... and they hated him and could not speak words of peace to him."

After years of failure, we might expect Yosef to have figured out *why* his talents didn't bear fruit. But the cause of his failures was hidden in the one place he would never look: in himself. His explanation? "I was stolen from the land of the Hebrews, and here, also, I didn't do anything wrong, but they put me in this prison just the same." He saw himself as a victim of the jealousy or malice of others.

The key question is: Why can't Yosef come to terms with his own role in his lack of success? Why doesn't he know that he needs more than dreams and charisma? Doesn't he—don't we all—want to be more effective? All Yosef has to do is take responsibility for his own failures, and leading-Egypt-sized potential will emerge. A relatively minor flaw that has sabotaged his potential could easily be compensated for. The equation seems absurd—a few moments of vulnerability in order to actualize enormous potential?! And yet Yosef resists wholeheartedly. Why?

THE INVISIBLE DRAGON[5]

The simple, tragic answer is that for Yosef, and for anyone in the grips of shame, admitting wrongdoing feels extremely threatening. Shame magnifies a difference, flaw, or weakness until it becomes an indictment of the whole person. It leads a person to believe that she is fundamentally bad, inadequate, defective, or unworthy, or not fully valid as a human being.[6] For someone full of shame, being accepted or viewed positively feels like a possible lifeline of self-worth. A threat to that lifeline will therefore be met with an intense, dramatic response. Yosef's mother Rachel expressed this desperation when she exclaimed: "Give me sons! For if you don't, I am like a dead woman!"

No amount of rational analysis can convince a shame-filled person that her supposed flaw isn't all that bad. Shame leads a person to anticipate utter rejection if she admits to her differences or short-comings. It is built upon an *inner* sense of inadequacy or incongruity that often has little or nothing to do with a society's actual standards.[7]

People can often be unaware of their shame when they have achieved what others consider success.[8] This success forms an insulating layer around any shame. Take Yosef as an example: he was charismatic, visionary, and morally upstanding. He seemed fully qualified to be the next patriarch, the obvious successor of Avraham, Yitzhak, and Ya'akov. His success in Potiphar's house and his accurate inter-pretation of the other prisoners' dreams were further proof that he was the heir-apparent. Instead of positioning him for true success, though, his power sent him headlong toward inevitable failure, since he had every reason *not* to look at his own shortcomings.

Yosef couldn't hold "flawed" and "next patriarch" in the same sentence. He assumed that imperfections would disqualify him, so he refused to admit to them. He could never acknowledge the shadows cast by his own power—jealousy, alienation, resentment, and arrogance. He could not confront the reality that, despite his self-image (and ultimate destiny) of being a refined, charismatic, visionary leader, he also had a tendency to blame and alienate others. He was caught in the belief that it would be humiliating to look past his righteousness to find *self*-righteousness underneath. So he clung desperately to his defense: "I didn't do anything wrong..."

Ten years in prison gave him plenty of time to think and no one new to blame, so he eventually came around to confronting his darkness. The Mei Ha'shiloach writes: "After Yosef clarified the cause of the situation, Pharaoh had his dream, and Yosef was immediately saved." When he finally faced his shame, his full potential flourished. He instantly blossomed into a visionary and charismatic leader, guiding Egypt and the entire Fertile Crescent through seven years of famine. And, at last, he would then unite his family and guide them toward redemption.

THE ROOTS OF SHAME IN THE TREE OF KNOWLEDGE

Shame takes us back to the Garden. Before they ate from the Tree of Knowledge, Adam and Chava "were naked and they were not ashamed." And shame was the first emotion they experienced *after* they ate from the Tree of Knowledge of Good and Bad: "And their eyes were opened, and they knew that they were naked, and they sewed fig leaves together, and they made loincloths." More than any other emotion, shame frames Adam and Chava's transformation in light of eating from the Tree. What's the connection?

Rashi writes that, before they ate, they felt no need to cover themselves, because they hadn't yet distinguished between bad (which needs to be covered) and good (which can be left exposed). When they ate, they got a *yetzer harah* ('bad urge') which compelled them to make that distinction.

Shame doesn't happen until we start labeling "good" and "bad." Another Torah commentary elaborates: Before they ate, Adam and Chava did not distinguish between their genitalia and any other part of the body. Sex was no more taboo than eating. But having eaten from the Tree, they started dividing their world into "good" and "bad," and their genitalia were "bad."[9] Maybe it was the animal nature of sexuality that concerned them. Maybe they were ashamed to have powerful needs they could not control. For whatever reason, they felt compelled to cover those shameful parts of themselves.

The *yetzer harah* is usually defined as an urge we have to act self-ishly or destructively. According to Rebbe Nachman, it is not a flaw in who we are but in how we think.[10] The *yetzer harah* takes over when we think negatively about something or someone. Shame happens when we have that thought about ourselves and then take it seriously, mistaking it for the objective truth. When shame controls us, we hide (or hide from) what it is we are ashamed of. And then we develop a complicated relationship to its hiddenness, expending enormous amounts of energy to keep it covered up. This is what we saw with Pharaoh. Since his dreams, as reflections of his waking thoughts, were heretical and wouldn't have been acceptable to his advisers, he misrepresented his dreams to them and to Yosef. He didn't want anyone to know that he was trying to rearrange the hierarchy of deities to put himself on top. He even risked not having those dreams properly interpreted, even though the loose ends bothered him so much, in order to avoid having to address them directly.

REAL LIFE

In the Torah, shame is the root of all negative emotions. Shame and its assumptions about good and bad are deeply rooted, often unconscious. These assumptions compel us to contort ourselves in order to fit in to family, marriage, and society. In a wonderful chil-dren's story called *A Bad Case of Stripes*, a girl refuses to admit that she likes Lima beans for fear that it will make her unpopular.[11] She wakes up to find herself striped like a rainbow from head to toe, and the more she refuses to admit she likes Lima beans, the stranger her condition becomes. She returns to herself when she finally admits to liking Lima beans.

Shame shows up around individual preferences, failure to live up to expectations, and inability to admit our limitations. From the outside, though, there's no need to be ashamed of or to internalize other peoples' opinions—even if you like Lima beans. But once the inner judge has decided what's good and what's bad, we become defiant, blame others, or pretend we don't care. We avoid the bad stuff at all costs, even at the expense of a marriage.

SHAME IN MARRIAGE

One psychologist muses that "married couples can engage in the most intimate of human behaviors but not be able to discuss it." He concludes that there are powerful forces at work that make it painful for many people to discuss [sex] even with their intimate partner. Perhaps the most powerful of these forces is shame and its closely linked emotion, embarrassment, because of the way they impact on a person's sense of dignity, self-worth and either masculinity or femininity. He points toward the explosiveness and sense of indictment that can show up.

> *Several wives have reported to me that if they ask their husband to touch them in a certain way and not to touch them in another way, they react as though they have been insulted and accused of not knowing how to be sexual and masculine. In other words, the husband immediately feels a sense of humiliation and emasculation if his wife attempts to discuss this topic.*[12]

Sex, of course, is not the only place in marriage where shame takes the reins. Any time we have blacklisted some aspect of ourselves—lack of skills in the kitchen, inability to balance the checkbook, fumbling directions, losing our temper, struggling to uphold commitments—there is space for shame.

Shame also happens when we hide what we want, like those Lima beans. It could be about preferences in the bedroom or what movies we like, what friends we want to socialize with or whether or not we should pray together.

SHAMING EACH OTHER

Shame is not only something we feel. It is something we do to each other. In a dark corner of the Yosef-Pharaoh story, Yosef uses shame to control Pharaoh. While Pharaoh knew all 70 known languages, Yosef knew all of them plus one: Hebrew. Pharaoh prided himself on his knowledge of those languages, so he made Yosef swear not to reveal his linguistic advantage. When Ya'akov died, Yosef threatened to reveal his linguistic superiority if Pharaoh refused to let him go to Canaan to bury his father.[13]

Shame is quite useful if you want your partner to feel bad. Author Steven Stosny lists 25 ways to make a woman feel shame, including: Ignore her, tune out her feelings, take her for granted, criticize her spending, tell her to get over it, criticize her family, act like you are trapped in your marriage, or tell her she is just like her mother. A parallel list for men: Exclude him from important decisions, correct him, question his judgment, dismiss his opinion, ignore his desires, withhold praise, condescend, show little or no interest in his wishes, rob him of the opportunity to help, and disrespect his work.[14]

Whether we are acting from our own shame or shaming each other, the invisible dragon is far more ill-tempered and destructive than any other factor in relationship. It dominates our mood, drains our creative energies, and obstructs intimacy.

DEALING WITH SHAME

To overcome shame, we first have to identify it when we see it: Make the invisible dragon visible. We begin by noticing what triggers our emotions. If we are disproportionately upset by a situation, our feelings are likely magnified by shame. This reaction could show up as rage, passive-aggression, blaming, being closed off, or avoiding eye contact. Any of those reactions is a red flag that shame is nearby.

Once we know what triggers us, the next challenge is to admit it. It is probably best to first admit it to ourselves. Tell the mirror: "I am ashamed that I don't earn more money." "I am ashamed that I'm not as manly as my father was." "I am ashamed that I am a slow learner." "I am ashamed that I yelled at the kids."

Once we have opened the gates of admitting shame, it will be far easier to discuss it with our partner. It is smart to open up the conversation when we are not in a shame-inducing situation. At a time when I am *not* taking on a task I can say, "Sometimes I feel ashamed when I can't fix something in the house." Or when we are *not* paying the bills, I can say, "I am ashamed that I don't bring home enough money to support our family." What a relief! I have had personal experience with this, and it changed my perspective on myself. Suddenly the mountain was back to being a molehill.

Rebbe Nachman writes that healthy relationship can resolve us of shame.[15] It does this by serving as a container in which we can stay connected and keep communicating despite the heaviness of shame, which will show up for most of us at some point. Healthy relationship allows us to forge bonds through honesty despite shame. These bonds serve as a safe haven when the dragon is prowling.

SHAME IS CLEARLY A POTENT FORCE in marriage. But knowing why it happens, when it comes up, and what we do to fuel the fire can help us keep it under control and eventually dissolve it altogether. For better or worse, working on shame is not optional. It is a toll road with no alternate route. But the toll is actually an investment in our marriage that is paid back many times over, as it gives us access to the treasure of our true potential.

VAYIGASH

Genesis 44:18–47:27

Yosef's chalice was found in Binyamin's sack, so Yosef
the viceroy will take him as a slave. Yehuda valiantly
steps up and offers himself in Binyamin's place.
In response to this gesture, Yosef tells his brothers
who he really is. He sends them back to Canaan to
bring Ya'akov and the whole family down to Egypt.

INTEGRITY

YOSEF, ACTING AS THE EGYPTIAN VICEROY, has orchestrated the situation perfectly. His brothers are backed into a corner. He framed his full brother Binyamin by planting his precious chalice in Binyamin's sack. After recovering the chalice, he claims Binyamin as a slave. The brothers would have to go home without Binyamin, who had replaced Yosef as their father's favorite son. But the loss of Binyamin would bring their father the same pain as when Yosef vanished 22 years earlier. Out of love for their father, they decide that they must bring Binyamin back at all costs, despite any jealousy of his favored position. But what can they do? They have no recourse. They are foreigners, suspected of espionage, powerless against the second most powerful man in Egypt.

Despite this lack of leverage or even a clear plan of action, Yehuda, the natural leader among his brothers, approaches the Egyptian Viceroy, intent on somehow rescuing Binyamin.

YEHUDA'S STORY

He begins to spin a yarn, rewinding to the brothers' first encounter with the viceroy when he'd asked if they had another brother. They had told him about Binyamin, but told him of the close bond between Binyamin and their father. The viceroy had demanded to see him anyway. They went to tell their father and asked permission to bring Binyamin down to Egypt. Ya'akov initially refused due to his strong attachment to Binyamin, but then he reluctantly agreed. Now, if they come back without Binyamin, Ya'akov would surely die of heartbreak. Then Yehuda adds

> *I offered myself as a guarantor of the child's return. Please take me in his place as a servant to [you,] my master, so that the child may go home to his father.*

At this, Yosef breaks: "I am Yosef! Is my father still alive?"

Stunning! Yehuda gave a powerful speech, honorably taking responsibility for Binyamin. But he had no idea that this was Yosef, and couldn't possibly have imagined he'd have any sway over the cold, calculating viceroy. So why did he do it?

He did it because he had to, for his own integrity. He had to redeem himself.

Yehuda had never fully taken responsibility for his role in selling frustrating-but-innocent Yosef. Now he could make good by taking responsibility for apparently-guilty Binyamin. He could redeem his failures, including the time he chose money over morals by suggesting they sell Yosef (37:26). And he had shown little concern for Ya'akov's feelings when he engineered Yosef's sale. Now, he could atone by acting for his family's sake at his own expense. Now his father's well-being—"if [Ya'akov] sees that [Binyamin] is not with us, he will die"—had become his priority.

THE INSIDE AND THE OUTSIDE

Yosef had been waiting for the right moment to unmask before his brothers. When it finally came, there was eruptive urgency.

And Yosef wasn't able to hold himself back amidst those who were standing there, and he called, 'Remove everyone from before me!' And no man stood there as Yosef made himself known to his brothers. And he gave forth his voice with a cry, and Egypt heard, and the house of Pharaoh heard. And Yosef said to his brothers, 'I am Yosef! Is my father still alive?'[1]

Why was his revelation so explosive? Because it is painful to hold back, to be less than transparent with people we love. It's uncomfortable to stand behind contrivances.

Parenthood, for example, requires a considerable amount of holding back. As I watch my son grow up, I struggle daily with what to say and what not to say. Should I tell him what I think about his choice of friends, how he uses his time, or what books he reads? How hard do I push him to give more attention to his homework? I know that he has to learn these lessons for himself, but that doesn't make my self-restraint any easier. When I hold back, my outsides don't match my insides, and the tension is painful.

TZIMTZUM

We're not alone in feeling the stress and strain of holding back. The root of this phenomenon reaches into the very foundations of creation. Kabbalah speaks of a primordial *tzimtzum*-constriction: G-d intentionally held back His light, which had filled all of reality, to make room for the world, with us in it.[2] But the Zohar tells us that, despite the *tzimtzum*, G-d wants to be known.[3]

G-d holds Himself back and wants to be known. So do we.[4] G-d's *tzimtzum* allows us to seek and find Him in a more mature, intentional way.[5] Occasionally we do G-d's kind of *tzimtzum*—as parents, for example, when we make space for our kids to grow.[6] But our *tzimtzum* usually comes from a fallen place, from fear.

Whatever our intentions, *tzimtzum* contradicts our desire to be known, as it does with G-d's. We want to step out of it, to be closer, more intimate, more connected. We would prefer to speak our minds, to be honest, so we look for ways to emerge from *tzimtzum* whenever we can. When the right opportunity comes, we tend to grab it.

In this *parsha*, Yosef wants to emerge from behind the Viceroy mask. Yehuda's authenticity provides the opportunity. Like Yosef responding to Yehuda, we are given a chance to be authentic when someone we love is being authentic. Because they are acting with integrity, we are invited to mirror their integrity. Yehuda initiated when he said, "please take me in his place." And Yosef could then reciprocate—"I am Yosef!"

MARRIAGE AND THE MIRROR

In moments like this, we witness a startling formula: authenticity breeds authenticity. Our sages say it this way: Words that come from the heart enter the heart.[7] Moving beyond what holds us back evokes a similar reaction in others. We open each other by opening ourselves. In fact, the *only* hope we have of getting our partner to open up is if we ourselves open up.

How does an argument end? Maybe one person wins through sheer strength or stubbornness. Or maybe we hurt each other as much as possible and then retreat to our respective corners. Our *parsha* teaches another way: a fight ends when one of us stops fighting.

When that happens, it's over. The other person can continue to fight or choose to stop, but there is no longer anyone to fight *with*. It has become an opportunity to connect and to heal even if it is still heated.

WHERE IS THE WORK?

Is it worthwhile to invest hope in seeing our partner change, or is it wiser to focus solely on our own process? The answer is more about expectations than particular tactics. We do try to refine each other—we give feedback, directly and indirectly. We speak as honestly as we can, hopefully with love and compassion. Sometimes our words are effective in keeping the connection open, sometimes not. But we cannot demand and should not require that our well-delivered feedback be received. *We shouldn't let our happiness and the deepening of the relationship depend on our partner changing.* To whatever extent is possible, we would be well-served by accepting the work we have to do rather than listing out what our partner has to do. And it would be best to do our work simply because we have to, for ourselves—not because we think it will change our partner. Any shift in our partner is then a welcome surprise, icing on the cake.

We open for ourselves because we need to. We hope it will cause an opening in our partner, but we do not require it. We hope the relationship will improve accordingly, but we do not assume that it will. We willingly accept our part of the workload because that part of the workload is entirely ours. And if the relationship reaches a point where our partner is not taking up his or her share of the load, then that issue will have to be addressed directly.

CONNECTING TO THE SOURCE – TOGETHER

Understanding the phenomenon of reciprocal response may explain a strange comment from our sages about the moment when Ya'akov laid eyes on Yosef for the first time in 22 years. They say that, at that moment, Ya'akov said the *shema*—Hear, Israel, Hashem is our G-d, Hashem is One.[8] Why was he meditating instead of focusing on the happy reunion with his favorite son?

He had another concern: Maybe Yosef was still angry at his brothers for what they had done. Ya'akov himself might still have been angry at his sons for selling Yosef, as well as at Yosef for not letting him know that he was alive. By connecting to the Source—by showing his acceptance that the entire scenario was in G-d's hands—he hoped to evoke the same response in Yosef. If he could reflect peace instead of anger, then perhaps Yosef would as well.

The method here is important—he couldn't address the issue to Yosef directly and say, "You should not be angry." This approach usually calls forth defensiveness or some other form of reactivity. All he could do was exemplify the peace he had arrived at and hope that Yosef would mirror that peace.

When we are embroiled in struggle and are in danger of falling into a knock-down, drag-out fight, one of us can shift direction by remembering the Higher Purpose and greater context: "We love each other. This conflict is held within the larger container of that love." Our partner is then invited to join us there in integrity and peace.

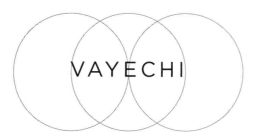

VAYECHI

Genesis 47:28-50:26

Ya'akov lives out the last 17 years of his life in Egypt, with his family intact. When he senses that he is going to die, he first calls for Yosef so he can bless Yosef's sons. He gives Yosef's second son, Ephraim, a higher blessing than the first-born, Menashe. Then he gathers all his sons together to offer each of them blessings and guidance.

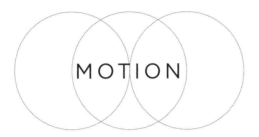

MOTION

REAL LIFE

Saturday night was a great night for Dad and the kids. They played games, munched popcorn, and enjoyed bedtime. Dad is on a roll, so the next morning he decides to take them sledding. He gets the kids all excited but sees concern on his wife's face, which he ignores. When she finally gets his attention, she mentions that Kid #1 has a birthday party at noon and that neither of the kids has boots that fit them. Kid #2 has been sniffling for a while and might be getting sick. Dad promises to be back in time for the party, lines their sneakers with plastic bags, and gives Kid #2 some Vitamin C. As we might expect, by the time they all return home, the kids are crying, Dad is frustrated, and Mom wants to clobber him.

Dad had good reason to believe he could pull it off—Saturday night had been such a success. True, he'd been on a roll, but the roll was slowing down by Sunday morning. To Dad's eye, though, each of the problems was solvable— just watch the time, use plastic bags, give a dose of Vitamin C. But if he'd considered all of these factors together, not to mention the concern his wife was trying to express, he would have done well to stop and reevaluate. But Dad didn't understand how "being on a roll" actually works. Rolls have natural peaks and ending points; they don't keep going indefinitely. Yes, sometimes an obstacle in our path is meant to evoke extra enthusiasm on our part, a push to keep going, but other rough spots definitely mean to say, "Stop." Knowing the difference is essential.

In the end, Dad's enthusiasm came to a screeching halt. Everyone was disappointed. But it didn't have to end so dramatically—kids crying, wife livid, Dad shamed. If he had stopped when his wife told him about the birthday party, he could have noted his tendency to make plans and promises without first checking in with her. If he had stopped when his daughter had a sneezing fit, he could have remembered that kids don't instantly recover from colds. He could have made a more realistic plan for that afternoon. Instead of going sledding, he could have taken the kids to buy boots, learned more about his tendency to push too hard, and avoided the disappointing crash at the end of the story. But since he kept pushing, he'd be cleaning up the mess, trying to restore trust with his wife, and picking up the pieces of his ego.

Dad saw life as linear. Running is living, stopping is dying—so don't stop! Dad has to learn that life is a pattern of living and dying, of running and stopping, cycles of movement and rest, exertion and integration.

A LIFE WELL-LIVED

The Parsha begins: "And Ya'akov *lived*." Biologically speaking, life features self-regulation, metabolism, response to stimuli, adaptation, and growth. But the Torah has its own definitions. In fact, there is a kind of angel called *chayot* that, in a certain way, is the epitome of *life*. *Chayot* literally means "living beings."[1] The verse tells us that the *chayot* are "*ratzo v'shov*," which means, approximately, "running and returning." All the major commentaries[2] explain this unique phrase in a similar vein: The chayot are in constant motion. Life—as represented by the *chayot*—is movement. To live is to move.

Ratzo v'shov is more than just movement. It is spiritual movement, within a cycle, with the goal of continual growth during all phases of the cycle.[3] Amidst the ongoing flux between these two types of experience—*ratzo*-running and *shov*-returning—growth happens. The better we grasp the nature of these two phases, the more we can live in a full, balanced, and healthy way.

To understand *ratzo v'shov*, think of an auto race. Two things need to happen for the driver to reach the finish line. One is to drive well when the car is running smoothly. The other is to make pit stops at the right times for refueling and maintenance. If both phases are done well, the driver will finish the race. But if she ignores the car's needs or, on the other hand, spends all her time in the pit, she won't. Driving is *ratzo*. Pit stops are *shov*.

The *ratzo* phase is exciting. There is so much happening. I love where I am going. I believe in myself. I know I have what it takes. I am inspired! My life is meaningful! Look out—here I come! That's Dad on Saturday night—effortless, joyous, connected.

And then there is *shov*. This is the time when I must sort my experiences, process them, and integrate them. Sometimes *shov* feels like work. There may be a part of me that I don't want to look at or even acknowledge is there, but *shov* requires that I do. When *shov* feels like work that we don't want to do, it is hard to motivate ourselves—tightening a screw doesn't provide the rush of racing. And there can often be anxiety—why didn't I resolve this issue the last time I encountered it? What if I can't figure out how to make the necessary changes? What if I don't know enough or am not strong enough? That's Dad on Sunday afternoon, trying to figure out what went wrong, how to fix it, how to make good. But that's only one kind of *shov*—the other is Dad taking a deep breath, letting go of his sledding plans, reevaluating, checking in with Mom. Shabbat is also *shov* (they share the same root), a time to stop working in order to integrate change.

UNDERSTAND THE CYCLE

Ratzo and *shov* get their meaning only in relationship to each other. *Ratzo* gives us a sense of what is possible, and *shov* points toward the inner work we need to do in order to get there. *Ratzo* inspires us to do the *shov* work when it comes. And the next *ratzo* simply cannot happen until this *shov* is effectively navigated. But once the *shov* work has been attended to sufficiently, a *ratzo* period kicks right in.

Rebbe Nachman challenges us to see that moving between these two phases is what constitutes "life." Only by moving through the complete cycle can we be fully alive and growing. Living only in *ratzo*, chasing the finish line, is not life. It is an escape from responsibility and a denial of potential. It ignores the depth that only self-examination and clarification can provide. On the other hand, a non-stop *shov*—obsessing over the possible flaws in who we are, ironing out every possible kink—is not life either. If we never see our talents in real time, and taste the successes that result, we may stop setting goals. Only when experience and integration, insight and application, life and examination are working in tandem do we have *life*.

Rebbe Nachman says we have to be experts in both *ratzo* and *shov*.[4] There are guidelines and patterns within each phase—things to look for, things to avoid. Once we understand how each of them works, we can begin to master them.

EXPERTISE IN *RATZO*—BEING A GREAT DRIVER

Ratzo is supposed to be a blast. We feel creative, joyous, free, purposeful, and capable. There is only one thing we have to keep in mind as we go: know when to stop. If we notice the need for a pit stop and slow down to give it the time and space it needs, we'll be back in the race in no time. But if we are convinced that this *ratzo* will last forever and ignore the flashing red light on the dashboard, we will crash.

We need to remember that any particular *ratzo* is only one leg of a longer race, so we will inevitably need to make adjustments. We can hold this view in our consciousness even as we press forward with focus and passion, petal to the metal. Insisting on continued external motion or even somehow finishing the race *now* will not do us any good. We need to learn how to let go of that pressure, which comes from both internal and external sources.

With that one rule in mind, go for it! You are not required to be who you once thought you were. Follow your gut, and approach people and situations in fresh ways. Trust yourself; take risks; have fun; reach for your goals. Remind yourself that you have so much to offer your family, your community, and your world. Just don't forget: it *will* end.

Messing up does not spell the end of the *ratzo*. You can tune up and get right back to the race. Did you rub someone the wrong way? Listen to the complaint; take whatever you can use from it; apologize as appropriate; make adjustments; and commit to being more careful. And then off you go.

So why does *ratzo* require expertise? Because it is scary to cruise at the speed of soul, trusting ourselves in the moment without over-deliberating. And it is tempting to forget the one essential fact—that it will end.

EXPERTISE IN *SHOV*—THE PIT CREW

Despite knowing otherwise, the end of *ratzo* can feel like a failure—especially if our self-image is tied up in reaching some real or imagined finish line. The desire for accomplishment and success can be very seductive. Bear this in mind, and follow *shov*'s one basic rule: sidestep those distractions and do the inner work, whatever it takes.

For one thing, *shov* takes humility. Even after admitting that we need to stop and repair, we may need help figuring out what needs to be addressed or how to do it. We have to be open to feedback, asking for it when necessary. And we might need help doing the work. Maybe getting help is part what needs to be addressed—it could be that we are in *shov* because we don't know how to work with others, and we have once again encountered our limitations. Someone who insists on self-sufficiency will struggle during *shov*. For example, if I decide to fix the leaky faucet but don't succeed in ending the drip, I may feel lousy about myself and end up in a painful *shov*. My desire to do it myself kept me from asking my neighbor for help—I couldn't hear the end of the *ratzo*. If I could have brought myself to ask, it would have been a humbling experience, but not a humiliating one.

Shov requires discipline. Unlike *ratzo*, which is guided by instinct and intuition, *shov* calls for making a plan and sticking to it. If, for example, we realize that our health is preventing us from thriving, we need to commit to an exercise regimen. Diet, meditation, rest, and self-evaluation all work because of the commitment invested in them.

Succeeding in *shov* takes confidence. Because *shov* points our gaze away from the finish line, because it can feel like a failure, and because it calls on us to be humble, we won't get through without believing we can become the person we want to be.

RATZO V'SHOV IN RELATIONSHIP

Ratzo v'shov are not governed entirely by our decisions. There are also objective factors that push us one way or the other—the seasons, the holidays, and the weekly cycle. Some couples enjoy Hanukkah but always fight before Pesach. For others, Saturday night carries us into a joyous *ratzo*, but the Monday morning grumpies make it hard to connect. Biological cycles, mood cycles, and work cycles all chime in—maybe we get tense around April 15th and celebrate when end-of-year bonuses go out. There are rhythms that affect us as individuals, as a couple, as a people, and as a world. To get good at *ratzo v'shov*, we need to take note of how all these factors affect us.

Every couple also has their own intricate system of *ratzo v'shov*. Clear patterns emerge, and every couple would benefit from getting a handle on its own pattern, since external factors can push us toward *ratzo* or *shov*. For example, do visits with family tend to make him self-conscious, ending the *ratzo* he may have been in? Does excitement around the holidays hit a road block when decisions have to be made, clearing the way for a rough *shov*? How does communication go during her period—are they able to gracefully move into a more introspective phase of relationship? Experienced couples know these things instinctively—"she'll be ready to talk in a few hours" or "I know what that look in his eye means." Couples can learn when the best time is to talk, be alone, wash dishes, make love, pay bills, or give feedback.

Whatever the cause, there are universal patterns of *ratzo v'shov*. Here are the common combinations of couples' *ratzo v'shov*, and some ways to approach them:

YOUR PARTNER IS IN A GOOD *RATZO*, AND YOU ARE IN *SHOV*

Envious? She sure looks good when she's in her groove, smiling as she meets challenges, intent and capable. Did you see how she handled that situation with the kids?! She is giving so much more than you are right now. What are your choices? You could try to bring her down, or start a fight. Or you could appreciate how radiant and positive she is. Tell her you are happy for her. Ask for a pick-me-up. The better you communicate, the better it will be for both of you. You can ask her to help you with whatever you're *shov*-ing about. Lovemaking in this phase can be quite electric when it is allowed to reflect the fact that one is in *ratzo* and one is in *shov*—and quite awkward when it is not.

YOU ARE IN *RATZO* AND YOUR PARTNER IS IN *SHOV*

You're doing great, but see that your partner is struggling. He is working hard for your collective good. Don't make him feel bad for not wanting to go out with friends. Offer a massage or to make his favorite dish. Let him know you believe in him. If he wants, give him hugs and attention. But if he doesn't, don't. Everyone does *shov* differently. Meanwhile, you have your own *ratzo* to attend to. You might not be able to share your accomplishments and realizations until later.

You have to be extra-sensitive when your partner is in a difficult *shov*, like Dad on Sunday afternoon. He might see your smile as gloating or judging. His shame will come bubbling to the surface, even if you are careful. Much of what you do can and will be misinterpreted at these times. Depression may be right around the corner. Let him know you see what he's going through and that he can tell you if there's anything you can do to help. And then you listen. It is *not* smart to point out what you think he should be working on, even though you might see it clearly, unless he asks. And if he does ask, choose your words well.

At the same time, your partner's *shov* is not your fault. You can be positive, available, and empathetic without taking it on as your job to solve his problems. Healthy partners don't get sucked in to each other's moods.

BOTH OF YOU ARE IN A *RATZO*

This is a blessed time! Enjoy it, and ride it while it lasts. Go dancing! Feel and express this energy as deeply as you can. If the opportunity presents, you can address areas of relationship that are usually off limits. The joy and laughter of *ratzo* can heal deep wounds.

I have fond memories of breakthrough conversations with my wife when we were both in an exceptional mood, alert and communicative, able to reach new levels of understanding and intimacy. This tends to happen with us around holidays or when we have satisfactorily navigated a sticky situation. What we share when we are both in *ratzo* tends to have a lasting effect on the relationship.

BOTH OF YOU ARE IN *SHOV*

A *shov-shov* can be as positive and impacting as a *ratzo-ratzo*. We can address core issues, make necessary adjustments, and soon be flying high. But if one of us falls into despair, it can topple both of us. If that happens, we would both end up clamoring for love and attention that neither of us has to give.

The same traits that are called for during a personal *shov*—focus, discipline, humility, and confidence—will serve us in our shared *shov*. We will need to filter out the distractions, like pressure to solve all our problems at once. Other people can be distracting, too. This is not a good time to socialize with people who don't understand the kind of work we are doing.

With discipline, we make a plan and stick to it. Once we have identified what our inner work is and how to go about it, we stick to the plan. If our schedule is preventing us from thriving, it has to change.

If we conclude that couples therapy would be best, we have to make it happen. If a one-hour meeting every week will allow us to figure out the budget, we need to set a time and stick to it.

Humility is essential. Two humble people can accomplish so much. They pool resources, drawing on each other's wisdom and compassion. They don't blame each other. They quickly reach clarity of action because they are able and willing to admit their needs and shortcomings.

Confidence is essential here. We have to believe in our relationship and the work we are doing to improve it. Our confidence in each other and our ability to move forward together as a team will give us the fuel we need to get through.

THE SEESAW AND THE DREIDEL

Ratzo v'shov can be quite dramatic. Triumphant highs give way to intense lows. Strong connection yields to exile-like separation, from the bedroom to the doghouse. The overly dramatic shift happens because we get stuck in one phase or the other. If we live only for *ratzo* and identify *shov* with failure, we will avoid it at all costs, and when it finally grabs us (as it inevitably will) we will fall into despair. Or if we so identify with our *shov* state that we never rise above it, we may not be able to recognize or appreciate *ratzo* when it comes. And then the *ratzo* might come out as an unhealthy manic explosion, a knock-down fight, or even a desire to end the relationship.

As we gain mastery over this cycle, the differential decreases, and we experience the transition between *ratzo* and *shov* as a subtle shift. Without fanfare we will welcome and enjoy each new period, with its blessings and its possibilities. Each phase is gracefully accepted when it comes and released when it goes. There is no unnecessary judgment of either of us or our situation.

Rebbe Nachman offers the metaphor of the axis of a dreidel, which spins through phases while remaining in perfect equilibrium, as opposed to the dramatic upheavals of the seesaw. We can see that a relationship is tending toward this phase when growth occurs with less emotional drama and less disruptive conflict.

YA'AKOV'S FAMILY

The Torah says that Ya'akov "lived" in Egypt. The use of the word "lived" in this context is rare. Ordinarily, a word liked "dwelt" would be used. The commentators explain that, in Egypt, Ya'akov was truly "alive"—alive in the way we have been discussing in this chapter. There's a great contrast between the seesaw drama of his family's history and his tranquil time in Egypt. But this tranquility was not because the issues that plagued the family from the start, such as sibling rivalry and favoritism, had suddenly vanished. They were still there, but they no longer caused violent swings in the family's mood.

22 years before, Ya'akov had given Yosef a unique, beautiful robe. This had fueled his brothers' jealousy to the point where they were ready to kill him. Now, when Yosef brings Menashe and Ephraim to be blessed by Ya'akov (48:13-18), Ya'akov again chooses a favorite by placing his right (primary) hand on the head of Ephraim, even though Menashe is the older of the two. When Yosef complains that Menashe should get the first-born blessing, Ya'akov simply says "I know, my son, I know." Ya'akov indicates a favorite. Yosef protests. Ya'akov insists. End of story. Unlike the way their uncles dealt with their jealousy, Menashe doesn't then go on to throw Ephraim into a pit. Last time Ya'akov favored one son over the other, it took 22 years and several near-death experiences to resolve the situation.

Similarly, at the end of Ya'akov's life, he offers his sons honest guidance, telling each of them about his talents and shortcomings. No hedging, no mincing words. This kind of feedback would have been impossible a few chapters ago. At that point, Yosef and his brothers were all blindly committed to their *ratzo*—Yosef ready to rule, his brothers ready to kill. All of them were unwilling to examine their motives or adjust their plans. Now, they are open to hearing—and *shov*ing.

Now that they are getting in touch with both their *ratzo* and *shov*, they are experiencing what it means to really live and grow. They are evolving from the seesaw to the dreidel. Ya'akov is teaching them that the challenges are here to stay, how to accept them, and how to work with them. He is showing them how to be in life together, with humility and joy. *L'chaim!*

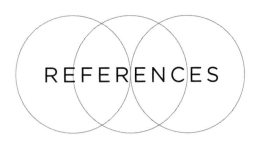

REFERENCES

INTRODUCTION
1   Gen. 2:24

CHAPTER 1 **TRANSITION**
1   Talmud Bavli Berachot 61a
2   Talmud Bavli Sanhedrin 38b
3   Genesis 2:19
4   A phrase coined by Dr. David Schnarch, director of the Crucible Institute and author of *Passionate Marriage*
5   Rashi on Genesis 2:18
6   Talmud Bavli Yebamot 63a
7   See Talmud Bavli Eruvin 53b

CHAPTER 2 **THE OTHER**
1   Rashi on Genesis 6:11
2   Rashi on Genesis 4:26
3   Genesis: The Beginning of Desire p.53
4   Ibid., p. 70
5   The Radziner Rebbe of Boro Park, Tiferet Yaakov Parshat Noach as quoted by Rabbi Tzvi Leshem
6   Gen. 18:23-33
7   Exodus 32:31-32

8   Gen. 6:8

9   Zornberg's translation of Midrash Tanhuma Noach 2

10   Maimonedes, Mishnah Torah De'ot 2:2

CHAPTER 3 **PUSHING**

1   Genesis 18:2

2   Rashi on Gen. 18:1

3   Rashi on Gen. 12:5

4   Degel Machane Ephraim Likutim s.v. Pihah, pri Haaretz in parshat Vayeshev, et al

5   Lev. 20:17

6   Rashi on Gen. 21:33

7   See Midrash Tanhuma Lech L'cha 12

8   Gen. 18:2-4

9   It is worth considering the practice called 'shomer negiah', whereby observant men and women do not touch each other before marriage, even when they are engaged. This is usually misinterpreted as condemning desire, but it is not so. Desire—chesed—"I want more of you! I want to be with you!" should still be there between people who are headed for marriage, even if they are not married yet. The practice is actually a vessel to temporarily hold that desire at bay until it can be consummated in a holy, healthy, and sustainable way. The same may be said about the time of menstrual separation called nidah.

CHAPTER 4 **LONGING**

1   Gen. 18:1

2   Likutei Halachot Even Ha'Ezer Hilchot Ishut 4 starting with paragraph 19

3   See R' Nachman of Breslov Likutei MoHaran I:31, I:66,

4   See R' Nachman of Breslov Likutei MoHaran I:66

5   Gen. 18:20-33

6   See Rabbeinu Bachaye on Gen. 22:1 for an explanation of the Akeidah as a punishment for Avraham's covenant with Avimelech

7   Gen. 22:3 with Rashi

8   See Midrash Tanhuma Vayera 22 and 23

9   Gen. 22:12

10   The difference between compromise and sacrifice has been defined by Michael Skye in his article *Compromise vs Sacrifice* as follows: Compromise - 1. Giving up something important to gain something of higher value, yet feeling like you lost. 2. Choosing between two values in a way that wounds your spirit, drains your power, and limits your vision. 3. Choosing from guilt, from fear, or from a position. Sacrifice - 1. Giving up something important to gain something of higher value, and feeling like you won. 2. Choosing between two values in a way that breathes life into your spirit, builds your power, and expands your vision. 3. Choosing from honor, from vision, or from a stand.

11   Heard in a class with Rabbi Gedalia Fleer, a well-known teacher of Breslov Chassidut; see also R' Shalom Arush's book The Garden of Yearning

CHAPTER 5 **HUMILITY**

1   Talmud Bavli Yebamot 63a
2   See, for example, Gen. 12:5 with Rashi
3   Genesis 24:11
4   Rabbi A.I. Kook Eyn Eyah, intro to volume I
5   Rashi on Genesis 24:17

CHAPTER 6 **MAINTENANCE**

1   Rashi on Genesis 25:20
2   For more on this topic, see Mei Hashiloach Parshat Chaye Sarah s.v. V'Yitzhak Ba
3   R' Simcha Bunim of Peshischa in Kol Mevaser vol. 1, Parshat Chaye Sarah para-
     graph 8
4   Genesis 20:2
5   Genesis 26:15, 18
6   Tikunei Zohar 104a, Pardes Rimonim 5:3, Rabbeinu Bachaye on Genesis 32:9 et al
7   Talmud Bavli, Tractate Berachot, 26b with the commentary of Rabbi A.I. Kook,
     Ayn Eyah, vol. I
8   As Rabbi Yitzchak Mecklenberg explains on the verse "And he called [the wells] by
     the names his father had called them," Yitzhak reiterated the names of the wells "to
     restore true faith to its proper place."
9   Genesis 26:24
10   R' Simcha Bunim of Peshischa, ibid., Parshat Toldot paragraph 14
11   Gen. 13:10

CHAPTER 7 **CHANGE**

1   Genesis 28:11, Rashi
2   Likutei Halachot Hilchot Hoda'ah 6:24
3   Sha'ar Hakavanot Keriat Shema 7 et al
4   Bachaye on Gen. 28:10; Midrash Tehillim Psalm 91
5   Exodus 28:17-20
6   Likutei Halachot Hilchot Hoda'ah 6:

CHAPTER 8 **UPDATE**

1   Beriesheet Rabbah 75:3
2   Genesis 33:8-11
3   Talmud Bavli Yebamot 62b

CHAPTER 9 **TIME**

1   Genesis 33:14
2   Avot D'rebbe Natan 6:2
3   Talmud Bavli Ketubot 62b-63a
4   Gen. 37:11
5   Talmud Bavli Yoma 38b

CHAPTER 10 **THE PITS**

1 Talmud Bavli Shabbat 21b-24a
2 Gen. 37:24
3 Ibid., 22a
4 Shulchan Aruch Orach Hayim 671:6
5 Talmud Bavli Sukkah 5a
6 Gen. 37:24
7 Ibid., 37:27-28
8 Ibid., 39:12-20
9 Ibid., 40:12-23
10 Ibid., 37:2
11 Rashi on Gen. 37:3
12 Ibid., 37:6-7
13 Rashi on Gen. 39:6
14 Heard in a class from Rabbi Henoch Dov Hoffman, based on *Mei Hashiloach* Miketz 1

CHAPTER 11 **SHAME**

1 Kli Yakar on Gen. 41:1
2 Gen. 41:17-21
3 See Kli Yakar on Gen. 41:1
4 Gen. 37:5
5 Name of Chapter 1 in Merle and Fossum Facing Shame
6 Ibid.
7 Merle and Fossum, Facing Shame page 5
8 Ibid., page 6
9 Ohr Hachayim on Gen. 2:25
10 Likutei Moharan I:49
11 By David Shannon, originally published by Blue Sky Press March 1998
12 Allen N. Schwartz Marriage, Sex and Shame on the website mentalhelp.net
13 Talmud Bavli Sotah 36b
14 Steven Stosny, *"Marriage Problems: 50 Ways to Cause Fear and Shame"* http://www.psychologytoday.com/blog/anger-in-the-age-entitlement/200904/marriage-problems-50-ways-cause-fear-and-shame accessed in October, 2010
15 Likutei Moharan I:34

CHAPTER 12 **INTEGRITY**

1   Gen. 45:1-3
2   Etz Chayim Heichal 3 Anaf 1
3   Zohar II:42b as brought in Likutei Moharan 33,37
4   See Rebbe Nachman Likutei Moharan I:49
5   Rabbi Moshe Chaim Luzzatto Derech Hashem Part I Chapter 2
6   See Rambam Mishnah Torah Hilchot De'ot 2:3
7   The Sfat Emet points to Talmud Bavli Berachot 6b "Anyone who has fear of G-d, his words will be heard." The phrase 'devarim hayotz'im min halev nichnasin el halev' – 'words that come from the heart enter the heart' is mentioned many times throughout our later literature, including Noam Elimelech Parshat Vayetze, Avodat Yisrael Likutim, Tiferet Shlomo Parshat Terumah et al. The earliest source of this particular phrase is in Ibn Ezra's Shirat Yisrael
8   Rashi on Gen. 46:29

CHAPTER 13 **MOTION**

1   Ezekiel Chapter 1. See Malbim's commentary for a lucid explanation.
2   Rashi, Radak, Metzudat David et al on Ezekiel 1:14
3   Likutei Moharan, I:6
4   Ibid.

GLOSSARY

BUBBIE – grandma

CHASSIDIC – adherents of a movement started in the late 1700's that reolved around joy and personal relationsip with G-d

CHUPPAH – marriage canopy, where the wedding takes place

DREIDEL – a spinning top used on Hanukkah

HASHEM – G-d; lit. "The Name"

KISHKES – guts

MEI HASHILOACH – a chassidic commentary on the Torah by Rabbi Morecai Yosef Leiner

MIDRASH – a creative rabbinic commentary on the Torah

PARSHA – weekly Torah reading

RASHI – famous medieval commentary on the Torah

RAV KOOK – the first chief rabbi of the modern State of Israel.

R' SIMCHA BUNIM – a well-known chassidic master

REBBE NACHMAN – the leader of the Breslov chassidic sect

REBBE NATAN – primary student of Rebbe Nachman, above

TALMUD – the main body of rabbinic commentary on the Torah, "published" about 1500 years ago

TEFACHIM – hand-breadths

YESHIVA – a seminary where people go to learn Torah

ZAYDE – grandpa

ZOHAR – the primary book of Jewish mysticism

ABOUT THE AUTHOR

RABBI GAVRIEL GOLDFEDER is the rabbi of Aish Kodesh, a different kind of Orthodox community in Boulder, Colorado. All of his work is infused with his genuine desire to bring Torah into contact with the real world, real people, and real relationships. Drawing from traditional sources ranging from Talmud to the writings of Rebbe Nachman and Rav Kook as well as modern psychology, his writings address challenges and questions people face in a thorough, engaging, and entertaining way. He has also written an experiential Hagaddah and a book about the counting of the Omer.

Rabbi Goldfeder coined the term Alternadox to express a commitment to traditional Jewish practice coupled with a wide view of Torah. culture, and world events. His website, Alternadox.net, features audio recordings of his classes as well as writings and links to his various blogs. He is available as a scholar in residence to speak on a wide variety of topics, and can be reached at heyrabbi@gmail.com.